Present Past
Past Present

PRESENT PAST
PAST PRESENT

A Personal Memoir by
Eugène Ionesco

Translated from the French by Helen R. Lane

Grove Press, Inc.   *New York*

ISBN: 0-394-17783-5
Library of Congress Catalog Card Number: 70–139253

First Evergreen Edition, 1972

First Printing

Manufactured in the United States of America

Distributed by Random House, Inc., New York

I

I search in my memory for the first images of my father.
I see dark hallways. I was two years old, I think. In a
train. My mother is next to me; her hair is done up in a
big bun. My father is across from me, next to the window.
I don't see his face; I see shoulders and a suitcoat.

Suddenly there's a tunnel.

I cry out.

: : :

When my daughter was two years old—on the rue
Claude-Terrasse—we went down the long hall one day to
Régine's room at the other end; she was sick and my daughter was very fond of her. Régine was in bed. I was holding
my daughter in my arms. Standing in the doorway, we spoke
to Régine as she lay there. We wished her pleasant dreams.
Then I turned out the light before leaving. Régine and the
entire room disappeared in the darkness. My daughter began to scream in terror, as if Régine, the bed, the furniture
in the room had suddenly ceased to exist altogether.

: : :

It was doubtless just shortly after the scene in the train:
in Paris, or in the nearby suburbs, in all likelihood in the
nearby suburbs, or so my memory seems to place it.

5

It was a summer night. With a sky full of stars.

A tall man, my father is walking with me in his arms. There are several people around us. He is talking to them. My mother is there too, I am sure, but I don't see her. In this memory I don't see my father's face either. I am looking over his shoulder. For a long time, it seems to me, a very long time, we walk alongside a fence.

The sky full of stars.

: : :

A dark room. The magic lantern. Someone (my father or my mother) sits me down on a little stool by myself, closer to the screen. There are grownups behind me. The head of the household, a man with a big black beard, changes the images. Are there other small children next to me on other stools? It seems to me there are. I see very clearly one of the images thrown on the screen: a little boy is sitting at a table on which there is a big cat with its tail in the air and all its fur bristling. The image is taken off the screen. I cry out: "Again!" This causes a certain astonishment round about me. Was this the first word I ever said?

: : :

A great deal of light, a great many colors. A summer morning. I am at the market with my father. There is a lot of green, lettuce, no doubt, and leeks. I still can't see his face; I am very small. I am walking alongside him. He is very tall. He has dark clothes on. I'm not sure whether I actually remember a market entirely roofed over or half roofed over, or whether I simply imagine it that way.

The light is at once very strong and dimmed somewhat by something that appears to be grillwork. Perhaps the light is also filtered through the leaves of the trees. I ask him questions about some very tall men in green smocks who seem very impressive to me. I point my finger at them.

It's because I'm so little, of course, that they all seem so tall to me. It's because I'm so little that all I see is pants and coattails.

There is a very fat woman near a cart full of lettuce and vegetables: do I remember this or merely imagine it? I am inclined to think that it is a real memory.

Then he is holding me in his arms at the market again. We pass by certain places that are still full of light and shadow. I doubtless raise my eyes: as it happens, I have a memory of a great many green leaves. And there is still the light, that the shadow emphasizes, that the shadow gives respite from, this light, this shadow, this coolness, this heat; I am still pointing with my finger, I ask questions, and he keeps explaining things.

I don't remember the sound of his voice. No, I can't hear it. But this time I see his face, a shoulder. It's all quite clear: he's holding me in his arms; I'm up next to my father's face. He's wearing a bowler hat.

This must have been at Alfort, or at Maisons-Alfort.

Maisons-Alfort years ago . . .

: : :

Was it the same day, around noon? We are in the house. The shutters are closed; it is cool inside. A square table; the white tablecloth. There is the same light and the same shadow as in the preceding image. There is the same heat, the same coolness as before. This is what makes me think that it must be the same day. The shutters filtering the light.

This room with white walls.

: : :

The same house. Was I three years old, four years old? There is my father. My mother is there with us too. She is in a happy mood. My little sister and I run around the house naked. The apartment must have had two rooms: we run stark naked from one room to the other. The door between the two rooms, between the two windows.

He and my mother are still at the table. Dessert. Cherries.

My sister has earrings made out of cherries. They deck me out in some too. It seems to me that I am kneeling next to my sister as she sits on a very small chair. I've eaten all my share of the cherries. My sister, playing a game, gives me some: one, then another; my mother, who is young and has black eyes, laughs with us; there is laughter in her eyes.

I am aware of him off to one side, or rather it seems to me that he is there, I feel him, like a shadow, towering above me. He watches the two of us play. We feel that the game we're playing is being encouraged. We play it another way, for them. We go a little too far.

A peaceful day, a happy day. We are all lighthearted.

: : :

There's another house. We moved often. In those days it was easy. Before or after Alfort? It was the house on the rue Madame that runs into the rue de Sèvres. The house is still standing. On the left as you go up the rue de Sèvres, the second or third street, it seems to me. I remember it well. The large courtyard with paving stones. They used to send me out to play in this courtyard. Immediately to the left is the dark, narrow staircase. I remember moving out of our old house and into the new one. Large armoires being brought up, filling the entire stairway. They'd sent me down into this courtyard so as not to get in the way of the big people, so as not to make things even more crowded. This building was very dark, the apartment very gray, very dirty. Still: it had two bedrooms, the foyer, one room to the right, one room to the left, and opposite the foyer a door

opening onto the kitchen? The dressing room? The bathroom? The bathroom-kitchen-dressing room?

I am in the bedroom to the left. He sits me down on a
little stool; he picks me and the stool, or perhaps a chair,
up and puts me on the table, perched on the chair and
perched on the table.

It seems to me that I am at a dizzying height. My sister
and my mother are not there. There is no one about but
my father and me. A gray light in the house. Yes, it is rather
dark; the shadowy corners, the walls, the furniture are almost completely black in this mental image.

It is curious: memories get darker just as paintings do!

However, I am sure that the room was dark; was it a day
in autumn? Did the window look out on the courtyard of
the building which is still standing, with its inside courtyard, and which I pass by from time to time?

Or did the window perhaps look out on a cardinal point
of the compass that doesn't get much morning light?

For it must be morning.

He is standing next to the window, somewhat to my left,
in long underwear; he has already put on his black shoes.
He is wearing garters. In his hand is an enormous razor.

He shaves in front of the mirror. Then he moves to another room; doubtless he is headed for the bathroom to
rinse his razor blade.

We talk together. I ask him endless questions. I wish I
could remember these questions! He answers them; he explains things.

I don't remember the sound of his voice; I can no longer
hear it. Don't we talk about the little boys I play with?

: : :

Two of my teeth ache. They are falling to pieces: an in-
cisor and a molar—a painful sensation. I look in the

mirror: they're decaying for sure; what a sad sight.

The feeling that I am beginning to fall apart. This is the last straw. I must find money for the dentist. I have to keep the cavities from becoming any bigger. One tooth goes, then another. One lock of hair, then another. Then a fingernail, a finger joint, a finger, a hand . . . Little by little, little by little we disappear, we come undone, we melt away. What remains can be picked up with a shovel and thrown into the garbage. Will someone come to pick us up, to put the pieces back together?

: : :

It seems to me, it really seems to me that the images of the village and of the mill are being erased, are little by little being swallowed up, or, rather, slowly becoming paler and paler, more and more withered, drying up like autumn leaves.

: : :

How difficult it is to forgive one's enemies. How is it possible not to detest them? And yet vengeance neither satisfies nor rewards one; what good can come of it once the harm is done? The harm remains, however, and that is what one must live with.

: : :

At the very last moment, when everything, perhaps, seems to be lost, we shall escape, we shall rise above circumstances, we shall overcome.

: : :

I see him with his sleeves rolled up, scrubbing my sister with a brush.

My sister is in the metal bathtub, in the gray water.

: : :

The other house. The one at Alfort or Maisons-Alfort. On the ground on a blanket near the bright yellow wall is my little brother Mircea, who died of meningitis at the age of eighteen months. The weather is warm, for all he has on is a little shirt: it is the only memory—and a very vague one —that I have of him.

Mircea is surrounded by his toys, or other objects.

If I remember rightly, the room is empty or has only a few pieces of furniture in it. How old could my brother have been? A year old, or fifteen months old, since he was able to sit up.

All four of us are playing hide and seek with him.

All four of us go into the next room. Mircea doesn't make a sound. He is waiting for us. We suddenly appear in the little doorway, next to the window: my sister and I first, and behind us, towering over us, our parents in the doorway. As soon as he spies us, Mircea bursts out laughing. I can still see him on his blanket, more or less stark naked, laughing and laughing.

We go out of the room and come back, playing the same game, several times.

He had black eyes. It was my mother who told me that Mircea was the only one of her three children to have black eyes like hers. As I think of this scene I see my mother laughing with the same laugh as my brother.

I see my father less clearly. Yes, he is there too. I must have been four or four and a half years old.

: : :

It is quite late now, since I am past thirty, to fish out of my depths, out of my cellars, this universe of light, this hidden, buried universe, or its glimmers of light: or these fragmentary glimmers of a universe. Several life cycles, several ages have passed over this age and buried it. This age is

more and more distant; it is now no more than precarious
flotsam, but the more precarious it is the more it tears me
apart, for it is now nothing but pale glimmers from a world
that once was dense, intense, brightly colored, and alive.
All this was centuries ago. I grasp only emptiness. Death,
death. Anguish over what is irremediable. I dig down into
an earth where I discover the debris of my prehistory,
debris that I can no longer make a single whole of. I
should have been aware of all this much sooner. Three or
four years ago my mental images were more numerous and
more complete. Before I was thirty, or at the age of exactly
thirty, I could still look into the valley from which I came
in a completely natural way, or, rather, gaze upon the sum-
mit, still not too far distant, from which I am now descend-
ing. Now that I am going down the other side—"nel mezzo
della vita" and even after the midpoint of my life—the valley makes the border of nothingness visible. Mountain walls
separate us from ourselves once we have a few white hairs:
they are the sign that the freezing point has been reached.
I have forgotten my childhood, I have drawn farther apart
from it in these last months than I have in the last twenty
years. I will not let myself dry up; I will not grow older. I
will risk being vulnerable.

: : :

We are moving to the house on the rue Blomet. My
father, aided by someone else, is carrying an enormous
trunk. The entrance of the house. Is there a horse-drawn
vehicle at the door? I am four years old, perhaps five. They
painfully inch their way up the first steps of the stairway,
carrying the trunk.

: : :

Still at the house on the rue Blomet. We have not been
there long, for we are still living in the little room on the

fifth floor, at the end of the corridor on the right. Later we live for a long time in the room on the seventh floor.

The image becomes sharper. It must be summertime, in the early afternoon. He has long underwear, shoes, garters. He is stretched out alongside my mother, reading the paper. My little sister and I are playing on the floor. I grab my sister's toys; is it a block? But I don't want to let her play with my blocks. I push her away. He puts down his newspaper and scolds me. I refuse to obey; I don't want to give my blocks to my sister. He gets down off the bed and gives me a spanking. To my stupefaction, my mother doesn't come to my defense. I am choking with anger, with helplessness. I am indignant. This is against the proper order of things. Ordinarily, I am the favorite; ordinarily, I am the one who is in the right. I swallow my anger, I rebel. I am very angry at him; I will never be able to forget this humiliation. Towering over me on his long legs, he gets back into the bed, very calmly, as if nothing had happened, and goes on reading the newspaper. I am still enraged, full of anger I cannot appease.

: : :

I often used to go for walks with him. I can still see his bowler hat. We often would take the little boat on the Seine that went from Alfort to Grenelle. I liked to stay on the lower deck of the excursion boat, kneeling on the wooden bench, my nose pressed against the window, so that I might watch, from the best possible vantage point, the wake that gave me the impression that the boat was slicing the water in two. I also remember greenish water. And an unpleasant light, one afternoon. Where had we come from? We were on our way home. I can hear the noise of the motors. He is close to me. I feel him, but I do not see him. He says something to me.

Another time we were going home very late at night. He is there on the little upper deck of the boat; my mother, my aunt are there. And other people as well, it seems to me. We wait and wait for the boat to dock.

We walk slowly down the steps that lead to the upper deck. It is dark. It takes a long time to dock. A dry wind. It is cold. I am very cold. I am sleepy. The boat is never going to get there.

: : :

At the movies. A film with a fire in it. I must have been about three. The film is red. Afterward we go to see my aunt. He carries me on his shoulders. We come around the corner of the rue Clodion where my aunt lives.

I am no longer very sure of the facts. Does a red truck with firemen wearing shiny helmets pass by? Is there a ladder? And do I ask him if the firemen are going to put out the fire in the film, or have I kept in my head the impressive image of the firemen I saw in the film that I ask him questions about?

: : :

I am with my father again, in a room, not at the house we live in. We have gone to visit my mother who is lying in a bed. A gray light, a yellow wall, the vague presence of my father. His dark silhouette: all he ever wore was black overcoats. People had bought apples and brought them to her. She adored apples. She takes one and bites into it.

My mother must be sick. I am sorry for her, I am anxious about her, but all this is mingled with a sort of repulsion. There is something that is a little dirty. My mother and he speak, I see my mother's lips move. (I now realize that this must have been when my little brother was born.)

: : :

At the movies again. I am between my mother and him. On the screen is the ocean. The waves rise and fall. The lighthouse seems to lean over and then right itself. I am nauseated. The storm, the fury of the water, the waves are going to flood the theater. I cry out.

: : :

Another childhood memory is linked to the preceding ones and it had a terrible effect on me. I don't know if I should talk about it. But after all, everything must be put into words. Perhaps this must be said in another way, in a "transposed" style, as the expression goes, so that the reader will not know whether it belongs to me or not, and will not know whether it is real or imagined. In the last analysis, very few things are shameful. All mistakes, if there is such a thing as a mistake, or incomprehension, or stupidity, all errors, if one can call anything an error, have an objective explanation and in the final analysis are not errors. We are all responsible, to some extent, for who is there who masters himself and his desires, who is there who can distinguish reality from a mirage? I nonetheless recount this childhood memory, for it undoubtedly exists and is one of the memories which has left the deepest mark on me. This memory not only determined my outlook on life; it is also the sort of memory that many people have, and it can show why so many other ways of behaving have been modified and determined at the very beginning of my conscious life. In any case, I cannot fail to recount it. I am thirty-five years old now. A few years ago I must have remembered, I know I remembered this scene in each and every detail. If many of the images that remain of my father, as I have described them, are silent, so to speak, in the scene that follows there are not only images but also the sound of his voice and my ear still hears my mother's sobs. It seems to me, and perhaps

it is only an impression, that the most meager details of
my memory are erased today, for since I have entered the
downward cycle of life the old inner world seems farther
away from me; it falls apart and lets itself be swallowed up
by fog. But what is essential in this scene cannot be torn
out of my heart. If I am what I am and nothing else, I
owe everything to this initial fact, or at least a great deal.
I don't know why, but it determined my attitude toward
my parents; and it has determined even my hatreds as regards society. I have the feeling that it is because of this
memory that I hate authority, that this is the source of my
antimilitarism, that is to say of everything the military world
is and represents, everything that is a society founded on the
male's primacy over women. My father will not be able to
read these pages now. I wrote, and published, a number of
very cruel pages about him. I may not have been right in
so doing. When it comes to a man and a woman, one does
not know which is the plaything of the other. Often it is the
apparent victim who is stronger than the apparent execu-
tioner. But it is hard to know what's what as regards such
subtle matters, and I get all confused. In any case, he and
I have each gone our own way until the Last Judgment,
and it is only then that we will settle our accounts and that
the misunderstandings between us will be cleared up. Today
physical and moral countries and frontiers separate us
(*1967: My father died a few years after I wrote these lines*).
Everything that I have done was done more or less against
him. I published pamphlets against his fatherland (the word
fatherland is unbearable because it means the country of
the father; my country, for my part, was France, simply
because I lived there with my mother when I was a child,
during my first years in school, and because my country
could be no other country than the one in which my mother
lived). He wanted me to become a bourgeois, a magistrate,

a soldier, a chemical engineer. I was horrified by prosecuting attorneys; I couldn't lay eyes on a judge without wanting to kill him. I couldn't set eyes on an officer, a captain shod in boots, without giving way to fits of anger and despair. Everything that represented authority seemed to me, and is, unjust. I have been judged guilty in a court of law for pamphlets that I wrote against the army and the magistrates of his country. I was proud of it. I know that every sort of justice is unjust and that every sort of authority is arbitrary, even if this arbitrariness rests on a faith or an ideology whose myths it is easy to show up for what they are. The new authorities are as unjust, as unacceptable as the others because men personify them, that is to say they personify their own subjective passions, whose theoretical objectivity doesn't fool me. The official position, the decorations, the honors, the reputation of such personages merely mask abominations and profound stupidity.

I remember that we tried to reach an understanding. I was eighteen or nineteen years old and I had left my father's house to live in furnished rooms. In order to pay the rent I had to give French lessons. That didn't make ends meet and I had money for food for only half the month. The second half of the month I went to the medical students' center where I had a friend who was a student on a scholarship. Students enrolled in the Faculty of Letters were not looked upon with favor by the ministries, and even though there were student centers for them they had filthy restaurants and dormitories where everyone slept together. But the students at Polytechnique and the School of Medicine had sumptuous living quarters: individual rooms with running water, and a restaurant with small tables. So I went where my friend, a future doctor, lived, and he provided me with bread and tea for two weeks. I managed to see my father two or three times during this time. He was rich. We temporarily fell all over each other, and he gave me money that I immediately spent treating my friends. Our banquets ended at dawn, and we all went home in horse-drawn carriages that wandered all over Bucharest leaving my friends off. I had spent my last penny and the next day I shut myself up in my room and refused to answer my landlady's demands that I pay the rent. Several months went by. I then met with my father again, and he asked me how my studies were coming along and gave me money that I immediately spent again, and so on. The last time I saw him, I had completed my studies, had become a young professor, and was married; we had lunch together at his request, and we had a falling out because he was a rightist intellectual; today he would be a leftist intellectual. He was, in fact, one of the rare lawyers in Bucharest who was allowed to appear before the bar after the Communists came to power. My father was not a conscious opportunist; he believed in the powers that be. He respected the State. He believed in the State, no matter what it represented. I did not like authority, I detested the State. I didn't believe in the State, no matter what it represented. As far as he was concerned, the minute a party took over it was right. This was how he came to be an Iron Guard, a Freemason democrat, and a Stalinist. As far as he was concerned, all opposition was wrong. As far as I was concerned, all opposition was right. (*Today, in 1967, I don't like the opposition either, for I know that it is a potential State, that is to say, tyranny.*) In short, at the end of our meals together, we were at swords' points with each other: at one time in the past he had called me a Bolshevik; this time he called me someone who sided with the Jews. This is what he called me at the end of the meal. I remember the last sentence I ever said to him: "It is better to be on the side of the Jews than to be a stupid idiot. My regards to you, sir." He looked at me with a painful smile and said:

"All right, all right," and I never saw him again. I was in Paris during the war and after the war. I sent a letter from Paris to a Romanian magazine, which brought down upon my head the lightning bolts of the press and the condemnation of a tribunal, one of whose members was his brother-in-law, a military magistrate of the new regime who had once condemned, a few years before, in the same capacity, defendants who were accused of being "Communist spies." My father informed me, from a safe distance, that I was wrong to attack the army because these Romanian magistrates were now the army of the people, because the Romanian magistrates were now Socialist magistrates. As a matter of fact, he now reproached me for not being a Bolshevik. Why did I have such a grudge against him? Wasn't he like everyone else? He has been dead for many years now. What I reproached him for, in short, was his being like everybody else. What I reproached him for was going in the same direction as history. But haven't Heidegger, Jung, Sartre, and so many others done exactly the same thing? He did so in a cruder, more simplistic, more candid way perhaps. Waves of pure madness swept over the world. In order to resist these currents, one must tell oneself that history is always wrong, whereas it is generally believed that history is always right.

He was like everyone else. That is what I held against him. That is what I was wrong to hold against him.

I must have been four years old and we were still living in the house on the rue Blomart. We no longer lived on the fifth floor but on the seventh floor. I lived in this room with my mother for a long time after he left. My little sister was probably in Médan, a children's home founded by Emile Zola, in his own home, it seems to me, which must still be a children's home. In any case, I am sure that my sister wasn't with us. I was sitting on the floor near the door. There was a window at the other end of the room. To my left was the bed, on which he was stretched out, with a newspaper in his hand, in a long white nightgown over his long underwear. I can still see him with his shoes, his socks, his garters. My mother was nervously pacing up and down between the bed and the window. I can see her silhouette in the light of the window. There was a wardrobe with a mirror near the wall on the left, and on the other side, next to the window, a dressing table. My mother is very unhappy. She is crying. He scolds her, he cries out, as he lies there in bed. My mother comes toward me, then goes away. She finishes dressing or else cleans the room up; she comes over to the bed where he is lying, speaks, goes away, grows more and more nervous. He does not allow himself to show any tender feelings. He has a very loud voice, an evil look about him. He keeps talking. What he is saying must be very harsh. My mother begins to sob. Suddenly she makes a move toward the dressing table next to the window. She takes the silver drinking cup that she has been given, in my name, the day of my baptism. She takes the cup and pours a whole bottle of iodine into it, like tears, like blood, staining the silver. Weeping the while in her childish way, she brings the cup to her lips. My father had already gotten up, very quickly, a few seconds before, and I can see him in his long underwear, hurrying over with his long strides and holding back my mother's hand. He calls her by her name and tries to calm her. My mother continues to weep as he takes the cup out of her hand. The cup, which I still have, is still full of indelible stains. Every time I look at it, it reminds me of this scene. My pity for my mother goes back to this day. I must have been absolutely astonished to perceive that she was only a poor, helpless child, a puppet in my father's hands, and the object of his persecution. Ever since I have pitied all women, rightly or wrongly. I have taken my father's guilt upon myself. Being afraid of making women suffer, of persecuting them, I have allowed myself to be persecuted by them. It is they who have made me suffer. I have made women suffer. Because everybody makes everybody else suffer, because everybody hurts everybody else. But each time that I have made a woman suffer or when it has seemed to me that I have made a woman suffer, I have suffered from her suffering. None of them has been the only one to suffer.

Today, years later, this scene seems rather ridiculous: it is probable that my mother didn't really intend to poison herself; she knew that he was going to keep her from doing so. This scene, however, is engraved on my memory and reason has been powerless to allay the fear she aroused in me at the time. This domestic scene has given rise to my sense of unhappiness, to the certainty that we cannot be happy. I still see her with her tears, her hair unkempt, her face twisted in a grimace; I hear her sobs.

: : :

We are living on the rue du Théâtre in the fifteenth arrondissement. I am very small. It is wartime. I am playing on the floor with soldiers that are not made of lead but of cardboard or plaster. He has just arrived by train. From Romania? I line up the soldiers; I have already broken the neck of one of them. There is only a dim light in the apartment. It is on the second floor. The window looks out on the wall of a factory. He still has on his black overcoat; his hat, a bowler, is on his head. He is standing up, my mother next to him. Is he holding her by the shoulders? He is talking quietly, asking me questions as I play. My mother turns her smiling face toward him and speaks.

: : :

It is in the building where my dead brother also lived. It is a small apartment, two bedrooms, it seems to me, and a kitchen. He has bought an enormous new doll for my sister, an unbreakable doll, because my sister has broken all her dolls. My father gives the unbreakable doll to my sister; my sister takes the doll in her hands, drops it, and breaks the unbreakable doll. I have a vague memory of my father walking off with his usual long strides, furious.

: : :

My mother and I have just visited my father who has been living in a hotel for some time in order to have peace and quiet as he studies for his law degree. An unmade bed. He is standing near the big bed in his long nightshirt, his long underwear, his black shoes. My mother and I are standing in front of him. She says something to him. He is in a good mood. Is he shaving? Does he have soap on his face?

: : :

In the street with my mother. An unfamiliar part of town. We are far from home. Why have we come here? I don't know why it seems to me that we went to the clinic where my little brother was born. Was he left at the clinic for some time? Or has my mother perhaps come to get something she left behind? Did she come to see a doctor? We are really far from home. She seems worried. Looking for a subway stop, for the right way to go home. Many white houses with narrow windows; lots of people. We are at an intersection. An anxious hesitation on my mother's part. Is she wondering how to get home? Or is something else worrying her? Her little face is drawn with anxiety; she is sad. We are painfully aware of my father's absence. Why hasn't he come with us? Is he still angry? Has he left home?

: : :

Several of us have gotten off a little train that goes to the suburbs. My aunt, my mother, my young aunt Cécile. My father apparently is not with us. I'm not at all sure of this. We are going to see my little sister who has been left at the children's home in Médan. She is three years old. So I must be four. A square courtyard, surrounded by low buildings with arcades. There are little pebbles in the courtyard. Nurses, in white. My sister suddenly appears before us, in a little pink dress. She is a little bewildered, a little surprised, and seems not to know where to go. There are many confused elements in this memory. This memory, these images are linked to emotional problems that I can't manage to get to the bottom of. Was she not used to seeing us? Were my parents ill at ease because she had been left there too long? Did I share my parents' discomfort in some obscure way? I know that we stayed there a long time. My mother, my aunts talked for a long time with a tall, overbearing woman, perhaps the director of the place. Many children scuffling with each other came out of the arcades and into the courtyard. The courtyard is full of children. I then see us in a dark room. Then out in the courtyard in the rosy light. I am alone with my sister. The two of us squat down and play with pebbles and the courtyard is big and the sky very bright. I can't understand why I feel so deeply touched when I remember these images. These fragmentary images must have been very important in my inner life. Why? There are things here that escape me. The colors of these images are very bright: sunshine, light with a rosy glow. The presence of my mother. And my little sister all in pink next to me. There is an indescribable atmosphere all around this image. How can I rediscover the meaning of this essential, indescribable memory? Everything has fallen into an endless ocean. There are only a few eddies on the surface. An irremediable regret. What happened, why is this image painful, why does this memory tear me apart? All the images linked with this memory are bright and vivid; there is almost no shadow, only a very slight one in the corners of the courtyard, a shadow where the arcades are. The rest of the images, the rest of the scene seems to have dissolved in luminous waves, in clear air; everything seems to dissolve or to have already dissolved in a blue transparency.

: : :

A middle-aged man with a round, reddish face and a little white goatee. Rather fat. At the table, dressed in a rather dark suit, he talks a great deal. A jolly fellow, a jolly Frenchman, happy to be alive. It is doubtless Monsieur Goton. One of the first of my aunt's husbands, if not the very first. We surround him. He talks a lot. Is this in Médan in a restaurant after the visit or before the visit we paid my sister? No, it was another time, or so it seems to me. We are around a table but it's the table of the little dining room on the rue Clodion. My father, in fact, is with us. We leave. My father takes me in his arms. I look over his shoulder and see the designs in the wallpaper.

: : :

One sees oneself seeing. One sees oneself amid things, among others, in a particular setting, an image in which one is caught, yet at the same time the image is outside oneself. The way a soul would see its life passing in review, the film of its life. I see myself playing. I see myself as if I were seeing someone else in my father's arms. I see my nose, my eyes, my arms. I see myself as I see him, as I see my mother, as I see other people. I see my back. I see myself walking. I see my eyes, my face, my own self with a hat on my head. It would appear that the photos that I still have of myself as a child help me to construct this image. It is as if I were someone looking at his brother.

Obviously I see better when I don't see myself; I see better when I see only other people: my mother drinking or trying to drink the iodine, my sister at Médan, the little boy with the clubfoot.

: : :

Sunday, in the suburbs at the house of retired friends of an uncle. They have retired only a short time before. Young retired people. We eat lunch in a cool dining room, for the blinds have been lowered. I am bored at the table. I go out into the garden. I eat all the strawberries. The grownups come out after lunch. They see the catastrophe. My mother, who is amused and touched, pretends to be ashamed. Since I am bored, they point out a little hillside I can go walking on. I cross a sunken path, full of shadows, and come out in full sunlight: red poppies in yellow wheat, a blue, blue sky. I have never again seen a red that bright, a yellow that yellow, a blue as intense, a light as yellow, as fresh, as new. It must have been the first day of creation. The world had just been created and everything was untouched. Everything has since gotten tired, all the colors have faded, habit has cast a shadow over all that. Our eyes have grown tired from so much light; we have lost paradise.

The brightest light, the light of Italy, the purest sky of Scandinavia in the month of June is only a half-light when one compares it to the light of childhood. Even the nights were blue.

: : :

Too late. In what depths can this buried light be sought? Several life cycles have gone by since then. Centuries and centuries. Centuries separate me from myself. Here and there is flotsam that is rotting and decomposing. Remembering, seeking things out in the chaos. I dig in hard ground in order to unearth the debris of my prehistory. A few years ago, three or four years ago, my memories were clearer and more precise. Up to the age of thirty-five, one can look back at the valley that one has come from. But now I am going down the other side and the only valley that awaits me is the valley of death. The mountainside separates me from myself.

: : :

"What are you looking for? What in the world are you looking for?"

"I wonder. I'd really like to know. I've forgotten. A short while ago, I think I still knew what I was looking for. I must remember. I no longer know."

: : :

I reread the pages that I have written about memories of long ago. At the time there wasn't much left of the world of childhood—a few tag ends of a world, and some debris. A few shards of a clouded mirror. I could still see my face in it. Now all I have left is the memory of memories, the memory of these few memories. I am trying to reconstruct some memories. There are memories as long as one's feelings still respond to the mental images and voices that remain with us. From this point of view, I don't believe that I am altogether dead.

: : :

1967: I can't find the rest of my memories of long ago. There surely is more than the pages I have come across in a little notebook because the last sentence on the last page is not finished and the notebook is numbered 1 . . . I may find the other notebook later, among my countless other notebooks. For the moment, it is as if the earth had been cut in half. I am on the seacoast of Brittany and I have the impression that all I have in front of me is a little piece of ocean. Where is the rest of the world?

: : :

What was there, what else was there? We all lose our memory. I seem to have lost more of it than others. Perhaps because I want to remember everything. Perhaps because I want to tell everything. I am not more attached to my own self than to others. My own world is not more important than that of others. Perhaps it is quite a rich one. Many other inner lives are even richer. It's not a question of that. It's a question of this inadmissible, unbelievable thing that my world may have been, that it no longer is. I am trying to restore a world by putting its bits and pieces together again so as to bear witness that there has been such a world. It's inconceivable that there is nothing left. I know: everything turns into something else. Nothing disappears, I am told; it is all one whole and everything becomes something else.

: : :

1967: I forget more and more. As everyone does. Am I going to lose my memory altogether? Is that what dying is? Even now when I drink too much I don't remember what happened, what I said, what others said to me, what I did. People tell me the next day. No memory, a blackness. But I have apparently been very lucid; I have said sensible things. I was lucid. I didn't give the impression that I had been drinking. I find this out the next day, I scarcely be-

lieve it, because I am aware that I no longer remember.

Soon there will be no memories. But it is not
memories or rather the conscious continuity of my
memories that constitutes and maintains the identity
of my person, of my consciousness. I remain the
same, with the same ideas, the same feelings, the same
reactions. It is obviously I who am speaking. It's as if
I had died several times over. As if I were put in a
tomb for dozens of years or for centuries, and then
taken out intact. From century to century, it's as if I
were asked the same questions and gave the same answers. The fact that my reactions remain the same is
like a sort of proof, a sort of immortality of my mind.

What if I soon had fewer and fewer memories, very
few memories, no memories at all?

Like a man going about with a lantern in the
shadows, lighting only a tiny space around him as he
advances. The luminous circle moves along with him
and all the rest is in the deepest night or goes back
into it again. The one ray of light comes from the
consciousness of a present, of an instant of wakefulness.

: : :

Morning, the sun shining through the fog. Night, the
road, the sky is overcast, no light at all. We are afraid of
bumping into trees, we're afraid we've gone past the road
that goes down to the mill. Another time, my mother looks
out the window, then turns around toward me. She is smiling. A garden, sand. A little girl with her doll. At school,

Monsieur Loiseau says to me: "You won't get your school certificate this year." The principal of the grammar school, Monsieur Robinet, who wears a black skullcap on his head and has a little white beard, says to me: "That's not too bad, but I thought you'd be a better student." Playing soldier, with my knapsack alongside me, lying on my back in a field, I look at a cloud. I don't know how to read yet; I am at the neighborhood movie with my mother and one of her friends; I take the program and ask: "If I look for a long, long time, will I understand the letters and the words?"

I can't quite explain to myself how I could allow myself to reach the age of thirty, thirty-five, thirty-six. I don't understand how I could have failed to try to prevent this catastrophe. Did it happen in my sleep? Was I unconscious? Did somebody get me drunk? A reverse metamorphosis: I became a caterpillar. Whatever became of the person I was, the person I must still be, the frail child, the brand-new being, and even the adolescent who still had something from his childhood left? Where have I disappeared to? Where am I, for what I see can't be me: already potbellied, already a bit bald, covered with hair, with my sweat, my adult humors, a ripe, overly juicy fruit, I who had such a horror of the gelatinous flesh of mature men and women. And a writer as well. Soon to be a quadragenarian. How could the Good Lord ever have allowed me to get this way! I am in someone else's skin, in the layers of skin, and the folds of the layers of skin of someone else. I have personal knowledge of the following fact: one can become someone else. That may seem absurd. The only thing I have left is my regret at being someone else. It is this regret that makes me continue to be myself, or the child that I was, that I am; oh, my colors, the colors of the world, my other heaven, my other world, my other oceans, my continent of long ago.

Everything has evaporated. I am on another planet, I look like a being from another planet; I was a man, a child, and a wicked fairy or an evil magician turned me into a bear, into a boar, into a crocodile—why have I been punished this way? Perhaps because I bit my fingernails or because I stuck my finger in my nose. The punishment is all out of proportion to the offense. It's a mistake, it's a nightmare, I want to be myself again, I'm that child . . . What shall I do? I wring my hands, I weep, I scream, but it's no use: they're really wicked! . . .

Far from us: constellations, the infinite blue sky, boundless joy, merrymaking.

: : :

There is a world. I can know it only through a self, the fundamental reality, even though it is a self *caught in the world*. I know the world as a self-world, as a world-self; therefore the world outside of myself, that I believe in but cannot know, is in fact the Kantian noumenal world. According to the phenomenologists, I apprehend the world in accordance with the structures of my mind: how are these structures different from the Kantian categories? (My mind = all minds = intersubjectivity.) Can there be a Husserlian apriorism that corresponds to the Kantian apriorism? Yes, perhaps, and this is what Husserlian logic is.

What is really new: one of the aspects of *this thing* reveals me, allows me to apprehend the essence of this thing, the essence of the Manifestation, and therefore what shows itself in the phenomenon. The essence of the Manifestation in relation to me, in relation to my structure, in relation to the structure of our mind. But the world in itself is not knowable. Because there is only *consciousness of the world,* which means that for Husserl, as for Kant, reality in itself cannot be grasped or is incomprehensible; it exists but it does not exist *for me.* What one knows of a thing is not its essence but the essence of its Manifestation, that is to say the essence of the phenomenon, not of the noumenon. This does not contradict Kant. It only contradicts the Skeptics, Sextus Empiricus for example, who concluded that it was impossible to know anything at all because of the endless variety of the aspects of a thing and the infinite number of points of view. For Sextus Empiricus, if one could know all the aspects of a thing one would know the thing in itself, for he did not distinguish the noumenal from the phenomenal, that is to say from the Manifestation.

First Tale for Children Less Than Three Years Old

Josette is already a big girl; she is thirty-three months old. One morning, she walks with her uncertain little steps to the door of her parents' bedroom, as she does every morning. She tries to push the door open, she tries to open it just like a little dog. She loses patience, she calls, and that wakes up her parents who pretend not to hear her. The daddy and the mama were very tired that morning. They had gone to the theater the night before, then after the theater to a restaurant, then after the restaurant to the movies, then after the movies to the restaurant, then after the restaurant to a puppet show. And they felt very lazy now. The lot of parents is a hard one . . .

The cleaning lady also loses patience. She opens the door of the parents' bedroom and says:

"Good morning, sir, good morning, ma'am, here's your morning paper, here are the postcards you've received, here's your coffee with milk and sugar, here's your fruit juice, here are your croissants, here is your toast, here is your butter, here is your orange marmalade, here is your strawberry jam, here is a fried egg, here is some ham, and here is your little girl."

The parents are sick to their stomachs because I forgot to say that after the puppet show they went to the restaurant. The parents don't want to drink their *café au lait,* they don't want their toast, they don't want their croissants, they don't want their ham, they don't want their fried eggs, they don't want their orange marmalade, they don't want their fruit juice, and they don't want the strawberry jam either (it wasn't even strawberry; it was orange).

"Give all this to Josette," the daddy says to the cleaning lady, "and when she's eaten, bring her back here to us."

The cleaning lady picks the little girl up in her arms.

Josette screams. But since she is a little glutton she consoles herself in the kitchen by eating mama's marmalade, daddy's jam, and both her parents' croissants and drinking the fruit juice.

"Oh, what a little ogre," the cleaning lady says . . . "You have a tummy as big as your eyes . . ."

And so that the little girl doesn't get sick, the cleaning lady drinks the parents' *café au lait,* eats the fried egg, the ham, and the rice pudding left over from the day before as well.

Meanwhile the daddy and the mama have gone back to sleep and are snoring. Not for long though. The cleaning lady brings Josette back to her parents' room. Josette says:

"Daddy, Jacqueline (this was the cleaning lady's name) has eaten your ham."

"That's all right," the daddy says.

"Daddy," Josette says, "tell me a story . . ."

And while the mama sleeps because she is so tired from having done too much partying, the daddy tells Josette a story.

"Once there was a little girl whose name was Jacqueline."

"Like Jacqueline?" Josette asks.

"Yes," the daddy says, "but it wasn't Jacqueline. Jacqueline was a little girl. She had a mama who was called Madame Jacqueline. Little Jacqueline's daddy was called Monsieur Jacqueline. Little Jacqueline had two sisters both named Jacqueline and two cousins named Jacqueline and an aunt and an uncle named Jacqueline. The uncle and the aunt whose names were Jacqueline had friends who were named Monsieur and Madame Jacqueline and they had a little girl who was named Jacqueline and a little boy who was named Jacqueline and the little girl had dolls, three of them, who were named Jacqueline, Jacqueline, and Jacqueline. The little boy had a little friend named Jacqueline and wooden horses named Jacqueline and lead soldiers named Jacqueline.

"One day little Jacqueline, along with her daddy Jacqueline, her little brother Jacqueline, and her mama Jacqueline, went to the Bois de Boulogne. There they met their friends Jacqueline and their little girl Jacqueline with her dolls named Jacqueline, Jacqueline, and Jacqueline and their little boy Jacqueline with the lead soldiers named Jacqueline."

While the daddy is telling his stories to little Josette, the cleaning lady comes into the room. She says:

"You're going to drive that little girl crazy, sir."

Josette says to the cleaning lady:

"Jacqueline (for as I have said, the name of the cleaning lady was also Jacqueline), are we going to the market?"

Josette goes off to do the shopping with the cleaning lady.

The daddy and the mama go back to sleep again because they are very tired; the night before they have been to a restaurant, to the theater, to the restaurant again, to a puppet show, and then to the restaurant again.

Josette goes into a store with the cleaning lady. And there she runs into a little girl who is with her parents. Josette asks the little girl:

"Would you like to play with me? What's your name?"

The little girl answers:

"My name is Jacqueline."

Josette says to the little girl:

"I know. Your daddy's name is Jacqueline, your mama's name is Jacqueline, your little brother's name is Jacqueline, your doll's name is Jacqueline, your grandpa's name is Jacqueline, your wooden horse is named Jacqueline, the house is called Jacqueline, your little potty is called Jacqueline . . ."

Then the grocer, the grocer's wife, the mama of the other little girl, and all the customers in the store turn to Josette and look at her with eyes opened wide with fright.

"It's nothing," the cleaning lady calmly says. "Don't get upset; it's the stupid stories her father tells her."

II   *Bucharest Before 1940 and Around 1940*

At the Augustinian Institute there was a lecture by Tudor on the notion of Man. It was only very timidly, very prudently that he dared to suggest that Nietzsche is in large part responsible for the fact that modern man, losing his humanity, has not risen higher, but rather descended lower.

(*I reread this passage from before the war in 1940 again today. The man in question, in short, was Hitlerian man or Fascist man.*)

In my opinion, he did not pay as much attention as he should have to Nietzsche's Luciferian pride. By wanting to become a superman, the man who harbored this desire became a hyena. I met Constant at the lecture. His gentle, tender, conciliatory air hides criminal impulses, criminal ones in the realm of theory. He came toward me, all smiles. I congratulated myself for being firm enough to tell him that his insouciant air didn't fool me, that the apparent friendship he showed toward me would not keep me from never forgiving him for his political ideas. He held out his hand, and I did not immediately take it.

"Don't you want to shake hands?"

"Not all that much, but since I must," I answered with a sigh.

Then I went with Tudor to his streetcar. When he gives lectures, he puts up a bold front: he is calm, serene, and seemingly self-assured. But in the street in the dark, he took my arm. He was about to collapse. He shuffled along with tiny little footsteps and gave a sort of plaintive growl from time to time like an old man, like a sick person. His life is threatened. My presence must not bring him very much comfort.

: : :

Before the lecture, Constant was having a discussion with a certain person named Virgile who has a graduate degree in philosophy. His face is the picture of decrepitude; he has a dirty gray complexion. Jean was telling me that Virgile had said that it was necessary to destroy everything so that everything could be started over again from scratch. Jean was stupefied and scandalized. Not me. This idea is by no means original, it is only a pitiful cliché peculiar to "revolutions" of the right or the left and does not correspond, somehow, to any sort of content; or if it does it is to a stupidity that is full of hatred, not to a desire for purification.

I look at Virgile, so ugly, so repugnant, so sordid that he makes one feel like destroying the world—beginning with him.

: : :

I plan to change my tone and my habits of writing. When I am too irritated, or when I am too depressed, I'll avoid writing. I'll only write precise things, note concrete facts. The least passion possible. (In the last analysis, as my friend C. told me, the thought that the mouths that speak, that hurl invective, that shriek insults will rot away, that the fists raised in anger will dry up, that all the sound and the fury will be replaced by silence, pure silence, the thought that no one will remember the tortures and the massacres, the thought that all that will be dust and less than dust, the thought also that what I like best in the world and jealously guard will no longer exist, that the arms that have held me, that have held others, will loosen, will unclasp, will fall, will disappear, the thought that all that, everything I love, everything I fear, everything I hate, everything I want to push away, everything I want to keep—when I think that all that will no longer exist, I am consoled, I can get to sleep. All that is nothing, all that is going to die, all that is going to be erased; knowing that all that is going to die relieves me, allows me to live.)

But I won't be able to write without passion, without pain, and without sorrow.

The notebook has two hundred pages. I have just begun it. What will our situation be when I get to page two hundred?

Where will we be? Will we still exist for that matter?

What is going to happen during these two hundred pages, I wonder with the greatest anxiety, but I hope that I'll get to the end of these two hundred pages, that I will still be around at the end of these two hundred pages. That comforts me. It will all be over one day, we shall surmount obstacles and come through.

Take heart!

: : :

I look these old pages over and copy them. It is hard for me to become absorbed in this past. Before I can tackle this block of memories, I find myself back in the present, in present events.

The Russians are rearming the Egyptians (this is being written in June 1967). After their extraordinary defeat, eighty million Arabs are encircling the Jews, we are told. The Arabs too will learn how to make war one of these days! If the Israelis are beaten, they will be killed. As François says, everybody can pity them from the bottom of their hearts. The left, he tells me, is willfully taking the wrong tack. It cannot admit that the Israelis were quarry, were victims. Thus there has been a reversal of sympathies. People are beginning to believe the Egyptians and the Algerians were in the right. People are fond of them, people like them because they were defeated, of course, but also because they're killers. In 1940, when I wrote the notes above and the notes below, forty-nine percent of the French were for the Russian killers, forty-nine percent for Stalin's Russia, which was congratulated for having helped the Germans attack the West.

People like killers. And if one feels sympathy for the victims it's by way of thanking them for letting themselves be killed. This complex, this state of mind is not so difficult to analyze now that we're acquainted with the various schools of psychoanalysis.

When I, who am neither a sadist nor a masochist, think that anti-Semitism is violently with us once again, in the guise of anti-Zionism, or hidden behind the mask of "progressivism" in the case of the Jews in Russia who have already been dispersed, I can't help thinking of what would happen if there were no more Jews; there would be neither Christianity nor Hasidism; there would not be, there would not have been either Freud, or Bergson, or Husserl, or Einstein, or Schoenberg. Not even Trotsky, or Marx. The most anti-Semitic anti-Semites are the Russians who claim kinship with Marx. But if Russia hadn't been Marxist it would nonetheless have been anti-Semitic. As it is anti-Arab: the Arabs are good for the foreign policy of Soviet Russia, but when they visit Russia they are closely watched and are not allowed to sleep with Slavic women; this is even more the case with the Negroes, the black students who have lived for a time in Soviet Russia and have borne witness to this fact.

I believe in the Jews; I believe that they exist.

When Sartre said that the Jewish problem shouldn't be raised, for the one who raised the problem was thereby already an anti-Semite, he was wrong; it was he who was the real anti-Semite. What is more, he wasn't too fond of the Jews before the war in 1940. To say that the Jewish problem doesn't exist clearly means, from the point of view of psychoanalysis, that one denies the existence of Jews, that one does away with them. I believe that the world would be a harsh, sad place without them. What makes us go on living? The hope that some day the whole world will change, that all this will change and everything will be fine and dandy. If it weren't for the Jews, people would not believe in, would not hope for the coming, the return of a Messiah who will bring salvation. We keep on hoping, knowing that the Messiah is behind the door; we hope that some day he will open it and that the world will know abundant joy. We all hope in the Ideal City, that is to say, we all hope the New Jerusalem will rise from out of the desert wastelands and from out of death. We hope for the transfiguration of the world, and we will have this hope as long as this myth that comes to us from the Jews endures. Marx was able to modernize this ancient myth of the Ideal City.

: : :

This anxiety that I have all the time grips me by the throat. How can it be that I still am afraid of death, how can it be that I do not yet fervently desire it?

: : :

I have always tried to believe in God. I'm not naive enough, not subtle enough. A certain inaptitude for metaphysics.

But I have not altogether cut off the bridges to God.

: : :

At La Chapelle-Anthenaise, with Marie, I often went to Papa Dalibart's farm. We often came home late at night. Once it was very dark. We didn't have a lantern; the wind was whistling in the trees. Marie said that it was a voice talking to us that we couldn't understand; it was so dark we were afraid we'd fall in the ditch, that we'd bump into tree trunks, that we'd get scratched by the thorny hedges. When we got to the end of the field, on the crest that overlooks the mill, we saw the faint glimmers of light from our house down below in the valley. We were cold, we hurried through the darkness, we were almost there. We walked down the last little incline and heard the faint murmur of our brook. We crossed the plank that serves as a bridge. We went by the stable; the cows heard us and mooed: the smell of milk, of cows, of manure; we went into the house; Mama Jeanette's soup had been waiting in the pot for us for a long time . . .

: : :

I wonder how we are going to be able to escape. There is a threat in our skies.

Danger is approaching, encircling us, squeezing tighter and tighter. Will we be crushed? How can we resist and endure, morally speaking, how can we remain confident, how can we not give up, how can we believe in justice? Even if

I resisted, even if I were able to write books one day, to manage to express myself publicly, will I be listened to attentively enough, will people believe me, will they be moved? In any case, I won't be able to stand up to time, I won't be able to resist the centuries. At the very most, I may save my personal life in this deluge. But I will not be able to save, along with the moral codes I believe in, the culture I cling to.

: : :

Only those who have something to say should speak and write. Everybody has something to say. I am everybody or a part of everybody. I have something to say. This is not altogether true: those who are only everybody have nothing to say since everybody says the same thing they would say. One must be half everybody, that is to say, a little bit everybody, half others, half oneself. "Everybody" is the impersonal pronoun "one": it is mere emptiness. It is necessary to be personal. My self is what is opposed to others; others are those who oppose my self. It is this opposition, this balance that constitutes the personal.

I must try to speak and "speak myself." That is what realizing oneself is. To realize oneself is to exist. There is no need to be a great ideologue; there will be enough of them after this war, too many "thinkers," that is to say the sort of people who draw conclusions about the future of a past that no longer can be the future. What will come round once more in the future of this past will no longer be familiar. One must be oneself. When a person wants to be himself, he must not fear being banal, in order that he may be representative. Everything that may seem banal or superficial or dull may become exciting, astonishing, in twenty or fifty years.

One must look at things from a great height. One must not let oneself be caught in the trap of ideologies, the ephemeral clichés, the circumscribed truths of the day, those that would have it, for example, that individualist literature is out of date; that it is necessary to write in a "collectivist" spirit in order to express the nationalist or Communist or Nazi world or some other. (As a matter of fact, it is ideologies and ideological literatures, ideological fashions that are perishable; today, in 1967, we see this to be true as regards the ideological fashions of twenty-five or thirty years ago, but people are not yet aware that the ideological fashions of today are as perishable as those of 1935. What is left of Fascist doctrines? But writers remain. Brunetière or Taine are no longer worth reading as critics. But the writers that they judged, favorably or unfavorably, continue to exist. Yet Brunetière or Sainte-Beuve—exactly like Taine, exactly like Goldmann, exactly like Barthes or Dort today—attempted to guide literature with the same dogmatic self-importance. On the other hand, when individualism in literature is condemned, or was condemned, did people realize, or do they realize today that individualism perhaps does not exist, that it is only a way of expressing others by way of the self?)

It is necessary to be above all that, to soar above one's time, to go beyond it so as not to disappear with it. It is perhaps because I am weak, or because I am strong, for what appears to be a weakness may be a strength, that I am going to be able to resist the crises, the currents, the ebb and flow of time, not outside of my time but struggling with my time, going against the current, opposing my time and expressing it through this very opposition to it. This opposition does not manifest itself in ideologies, for ideologies are only waves that are destined to disappear. I will not be another wave, but a rock, perhaps, that is to say a human permanence, a sort of universal consciousness, something covered up by the waves, but still there nonetheless. One must not let oneself float with the tide. One must retain one's lucidity, not be a dupe, judge things sensibly; ideologies are mad, everybody is an ideologue, everybody is passionately, fanatically ideological; what the ideologues call "common" sense is often the "exceptional" sense that they lack. Ideologies are crises.

And if I manage to acquire a name for myself, this will be both something important and something not very important at all. Chance may cause what I write to meet with a favorable moment, a time neither too close at hand, when the storm is still raging, nor too far away, when the storm will have been over for too long a time. And if I were to succeed in finding a posterity to welcome me, what would it matter? It isn't worth the trouble. The only concern that makes a man rise above himself is a concern for the absolute, I mean the yearning, the essential desire for the absolute. Our era is an era that has declined, for the political problem, the furor over politics has taken the place of preoccupation with the absolute. When man no longer bothers about the problems of ultimate ends, when only the destiny of a political nation, of an economic system interests him, when the great metaphysical problems no longer cause man to suffer and leave him indifferent, humanity is degraded and becomes bestial. Nothing seems more lamentably stupid than to sell one's life to some common, ordinary political party. Let us be on our guard against the lie that would have it that what is political is also spiritual and that politics too is a metaphysical answer.

Politics are no longer the organization of the City, they are the disorganization of the City, they are a desire to turn things upside down and to destroy, they are disorder for the sake of disorder, revolution for the sake of revolution; they are a hidden wish to blot out the accomplishments of the spirit: unstable revolutions, tyrannies and systems of censorship, cultural revolutions are the destruction of culture; cultural revolutions burn books, destroy monuments. We see this in our own day too, in 1967, when interdictions are rife, as in the time of Savonarola. Modern revolutions with their false religions are like the Christian revolutions that destroyed cultures; they are like the Moslem faith that destroyed Byzantium and the monuments of Athens. All revolutions destroy libraries of Alexandria.

: : :

The "esthetic" point of view is equally undistinguished. For the angels, for the divine consciousness, or for the spirit, the supreme intelligence, cathedrals are mere crude piles of stone, vague rough outlines of signs, a clumsy language; even the music of Bach is something that creaks painfully.

: : :

In a year we will perhaps be dead, or perhaps the nightmare will have faded away and we will breathe freely. In a year or two, we will be lighthearted, we will dance if our legs are still young, if we still have teeth left, if they aren't eaten away by cavities.

A visit to B. The wine, the music, and a few paintings awaken my nostalgia for beauty, for adventure, for untrammeled freedom. Men discovered the Cape of Good Hope, they discovered North and South America, they discovered unknown cities, palaces, unknown fruits; they met men of another color and came across unusual civilizations. And here we are among the ugliest people on earth, among cretins, louts, ogres that are trying to devour us—what a sad fate! What have we done, God, to be in the hands of such people?

I live in terror from morning to night. At night I have nightmares—I who wanted to be a conquistador!

: : :

I am sailing in a frail skiff through the storms of chaos. The people I know all have a system to explain the world and everything that happens finds a place in this system. They all understand and can explain everything. I am the only one in the world who doesn't understand anything; they all have keys or passkeys.

All systems are false; that is to say, all systems are and cannot help but be merely images, different ways of imagining or representing the world, which is only the starting point of these representations. All systems begin with reality, which is amorphous, and go on from there. The more perfect, complete, believable, convincing, logical, and coherent a system is, the more unreal and artificial it is. All systems, therefore, are fundamentally artificial and far removed from reality. If we care to, we may choose one of these systems (two or three of them are common currency in the world), one of these images or explanations that suits us best; but I hate the fascist cosmos, I do not like, nor do I admire, the communist cosmos, and I really wonder whether I prefer the various liberalisms, those makeshifts! A man who cannot quite convince himself that the system does not express, does not cover, does not extinguish, does not absorb reality, the man who refuses the keys and has no passkey, can only live in chaos. It is not a livable human reality. I am amid chaos, I live in the unlivable.

In order to believe that what I call chaos is not chaos, I must manage to believe in a God who doesn't have any place either in any possible human system. Let us not allow ourselves to be passively carried along by the currents of opinion, the ideologies, the passions, and the fanaticisms of history. But let us allow ourselves to be carried along by the waves of chaos. Let us allow ourselves to go out onto this stormy sea, into reality.

: : :

I am beneath everything, I tell myself, But to tell the truth, I don't believe it. I am, rather, above everything, it seems to me. But if I think that I am below or above everything and anything, these expressions merely prove that I also have a system, certain sorts of criteria.

Not having a system is having one nonetheless.

I am only on the edge of chaos: I am not yet mad. Or else, from the other point of view, I am only at the edge of chaos: I am still mad. To be mad is to have a representation of the world, to provide oneself with explanations. Men are mad. To say that I am not a madman is to say that I am mad in men's eyes. I am only *almost* mad. My mind still *organizes,* though in a very simplistic fashion.

: : :

I go over these notes of more than a quarter of a century ago. I note once again how little I have changed. And as usual I am at odds with myself. (I'm going to end up admiring myself!) I can't help coming back to the present: Clostermann, in the *Figaro littéraire,* gives an admirable account of how the Egyptians, and not the Jews, were the aggressors in the recent war against Israel. It so happens that before Israel attacked Egyptian tanks were stationed in Sinai, then farther from the coast, spread out over several dozen kilometers, in Israeli territory. Israeli radar had revealed the presence of more than a hundred Egyptian planes. Israel really held back, at the risk of her life, up until the very last moment, before taking action.

Certain French Jews, intellectuals spoiled by leftism, have been writing letters in the papers saying that the very presence of Jews in Palestine was an act of aggression against the Arabs. They perfidiously support the views of the Arabs who will not be grateful to them for this. They are like the Jews who wanted to collaborate with the Nazis and were massacred. If to occupy a territory is to commit an act of aggression, then everything is an aggression: the French are aggressors in Corsica, in Britanny, in Languedoc. The Algerians themselves are aggressors in Algeria, since they came from somewhere else. The whole European continent is occupied by "aggressors" from Iran and Asia. For those Jews who are members of the Communist party, there is apparently such a thing as property on this earth. This is odd, coming from Communists . . .

In reality, the whole earth belongs to everyone, it belongs to whoever fructifies it, it belongs above all to those who ask only a little corner to live in without making war. The Algerian and Egyptian position is untenable. It was born, indeed, of envy. But who was it in the final analysis who asked the soldiers of the

U.N. to leave Sinai? It was none other than the Egyptians, wasn't it? And why? Doubtless not to attack Israel, doubtless because the Egyptians did not want to be defended, doubtless because the Egyptians wanted at all costs to be exterminated by the Jews.

: : :

Certain peoples live on hatred. There are perhaps reasons for this hatred, but it is time now to exorcise it because it alienates and dehumanizes those countries themselves. The Jews are not a people beyond reproach: there are the monstrous Jews who declare their solidarity with the Arab peoples in their "just" struggle, others who are the accomplices of the Algerian leaders and are not only anti-Israelis but also anti-Jews because they sent threatening letters to Israel to those who judged Eichmann. Yes, these "intellectual" Jews are really the sons of the Jews in Hitler's time.

X. says to me:

"There are no great artists, there have been no great writers who have been behind their time!" (*My comment today: In 1935 as in 1967, writers were asked to be committed politically and to go along in the same direction as the march of History; the same blackmail used by the Fascists, who also were following the march of History, today is used by the Communists, the Soviets, the leftists. The revolutionaries, the leaders, the agitators, the "libido dominandi" of today differ only in their doctrine, this latter being only the mask, the mystification of the same fundamental "libido dominandi." But I go back to the notes written around 1940, which follow.*)

What does it mean, though, to "be behind one's time"? This is yet another of the numerous clichés that we ought to erase from our minds, that we ought to refuse to use, but "being behind one's time" is often precisely to be part of the opposition of a minority that criticizes the march of the History of its time and the direction it is taking. To "be behind the times" really means "not going along," "not getting trapped"; one more or less has the impression that there are no stragglers and no precursors: but it is as if there were certain principles or attitudes or permanent positions, waging a permanent struggle, that are alternately taken up and rejected, alternately defeated or victorious, whose different aspects, varying according to the particular historical period, are not essential, but whose profound identity is essential. Kant takes up Plato's ideas again; in his way, Jung's archetypes also are a new justification of Plato's ideas. Bergson takes up Heraclitus again, as did Hegel. (*The various theories of structuralism also espouse immutabilities that are opposed to the theories of change and evolution.*)

Democratic societies succeed aristocratic societies; tyrannies succeed liberalism; when a society, a social regime gives way, reaction or revolution, two terms which at bottom may be synonymous, reestablish authority by the use of force, and so on. So that all those who oppose what is called the "historical moment" may be considered either "stragglers" or "precursors."

Charles Baudelaire, the adversary of the progressivist thought of the nineteenth century and of positivism, *rationalism,* and progressivist social reforms, for he considered that this progressivism was *regressivist* metaphysically, was in fact a partisan, a representative of an aristocratic attitude. It is he who is the author of the celebrated phrase that said that "The priest, the soldier, and the poet alone deserve respect, the rest of humanity deserving only the whip"; he was really "reactionary," a nonconformist, a paradoxical, isolated man, a straggler. At the same time he can be considered to be a precursor of certain Nietzschian doctrines in contemporary, very contemporary German thought, whether Hitlerian or Spenglerian: I am thinking not only of the Spengler of *The Decline of the West;* I am thinking in particular of the Spengler of *The Decisive Years,* that violent pamphlet against the "masses," the nonelite.

Baudelaire's attitude was shared by Edgar Poe who lived in democratic America: Poe too was against his time.

But there was no one more "reactionary," more behind his time, than Dante, the enemy of the Renaissance, of the young Italian republics, of nationalism, a partisan of the Hohenstaufen; didn't he desire a new universal European empire, and wasn't Petrarch also a straggler, since he wanted to restore the Roman Empire, and couldn't Aristotle be proclaimed a precursor by today's racists who were once considered to be behind their time but today seem to be the representatives of History on the march? But this march will be halted. They will become reactionaries again.

And I will perhaps be right again. I have a tendency, almost always, to be against my time, to be swimming against the stream.

I believe that our ideas are not "historical," that they do not represent a certain historical moment, or that they do not represent only their respective historical moment; I believe that they express profound extrahistorical tendencies which go beyond us and lie below the surface of History, that come to us from far, far off. Though they are in disrepute today, repressed today, they will reappear tomorrow, will crystallize tomorrow in another way, and resume the struggle. Ideas, in reality, are the expression of tendencies that are not merely mental and social; they are the expression, so to speak, of metaphysical temperaments. Biological and metaphysical temperaments. Biological, metaphysical, and cosmic. A little like the ebb and flow of the tides; like the phases of the moon, like day and night, like the seasons that come and go, that seem to chase each other away. We are not alone; what we think is eternal. What I think, what I feel, others think and feel. Others in the future will think and feel it. Every attitude is justified because it is not the expression, the invention of any single individual; it does not express one case, it expresses a generality. Our ideas and our tendencies do not go astray, do not wither away. We should try to define these eternal principles that we rediscover in all these different aspects at every moment of History. Nonetheless we represent our time even if we are against it; the movement is not linear.

: : :

To be free, to be outside of History, not to be part of the order of the world, not to be an instrument in the orchestra or a note in the symphony. Not to be onstage. To see and hear everything from the audience. As if one were outside the universe. If we are onstage, if we are part of the orchestra, we hear only the tumult, we are aware only of the dissonances.

: : :

Just look at them; just listen to them. They do not avenge themselves, they punish. They do not kill; they defend themselves: defense is legitimate. They do not hate, they do not persecute; they render justice. They want neither to conquer nor to dominate; they want to organize the world. They do not want to drive out the tyrants to take their place; they want to establish real order. They wage only holy wars. They have hands full of blood, they are hideous, they are fierce, they have the heads of animals, they wallow in the mud, they scream.

I do not want to live with these madmen; I am not part of their festivities; they try to drag me along with them by force. There is no time to explain to them. So I too am a martyr who aspires to become a hangman.

: : :

I met T. He confessed to me that he believes in the transmigration of souls. He was having an attack of sciatica and for the moment could not even make it from one chair to the other. He is writing a theory of values.

: : :

Hitler gave a speech yesterday at the Reichstag which has of course been reproduced, as usual, in all the papers in the country. There is, among other things, a résumé, a statement of the ideas, of the metaphysics of German racism. Hitler believes in it or doesn't believe in it. But if History continues to go along in Hitler's direction all peoples and all ideologues will adopt these "ideas," which will become dogmas, the axioms on which a new science of man will be founded. Anything can be supported, anything can be proven by the sciences. People do what they please with science.

:::

S. says to me as he walks on the street with me: "Look at them, look at them, they are full of the mud of propaganda, they think they have invented and thought what has been stuffed into their skulls. In a few years, when the march of History takes another direction, their heads will be full of the mud of another kind of propaganda. There are a few who dominate: all the others are dominated, passive, as in many animal societies, many insect societies. But those who dominate are merely unconsciously obeying their instincts to dominate. Free men are not dominated, and do not dominate."

:::

It's all over, perhaps, for the white race. Some people say so, and I am inclined to believe it. If only this were the end, ah if only this were the end of those unbelieving but credulous Frenchmen, those dissolute Italians, those fierce, stupid Germans, those Englishmen who are sometimes mad and sometimes apathetic, those idiotically optimistic Americans, those cruel and mystic Russians who are mystics who worship what? Mystics who worship cruelty. The greedy Jews. May the yellow race run over these narrow-minded Westerners. The moment is not very far off. If the Japanese get supremacy on the sea, they will be the masters of the world. Hitler will have been had! We can be the white slaves of the Chinese and Japanese. Europe, which invented History, will have to drop out of it "for a thousand years."

:::

I could live just as well in the greatest peace. Let fatigue come. Ah, this life that we have such a horror of and such a fear of leaving! If only I were able to die without hatred, if only I were able to separate myself from this world, sadly, and still remain its friend, as we separate from the woman who has made us suffer but against whom we no longer harbor any resentment. If only I were able to overlook, to forgive everything. Even the mass slaughter that God, that History, that stupidity, that reason have permitted . . . It is late; I am too sleepy.

: : :

1967: C. said to me today more or less what I had been telling myself and continue to tell myself: "Don't worry about History. You must concern yourself only with metaphysics. History is bad theater. History is stupid and vulgar, it is the unleashing of the most sordid, the most misleading passions."

: : :

There are two races of men: those who are indifferent to the problems of religion, of metaphysics, of death, and those whom political problems leave indifferent or might leave indifferent. Politicians don't think about death; action situates them in a perpetual present.

: : :

"Why are you afraid of death?" B. asks me. "It's a petty individual problem."

Man in fact is petty: the problem of death is a human problem. A cow doesn't think about death. A cow isn't petty.

: : :

1967: For the majority of Moderns, metaphysics has become inacceptable, something to be rejected. It is because they are afraid that metaphysics might lead us to God. People are afraid of being alienated by God. But God, or "what is behind everything," is precisely the vital sap, the power, the universal energy that we partake of and participate in.

However, what there is "behind" is the one who, or that which, produces this energy. In any case there is behind me, the individual, something that seems to alienate us: the organization of society. Thus for the individual, let us say for the individual soul, there is no recourse beyond the organization of society, since the organization of society transcends me. There really is a transcendence, however much one may wish to deny this. In fact, we situate this transcendence elsewhere, on a lower order of things, I would say. It nonetheless seems clear to me that if I am moved or determined by the organization of society the social itself can only be determined by biology or by the mechanics of the universe, or by a universal consciousness, or by universal movement.

: : :

The Self is an illusion. It therefore exists—as an illusion. The illusion exists in the spirit, like all the rest. The Self therefore exists. The Self is a structural form. It is a particular sort of structural form. It is the structural form of this particular being, not of some other being. The Self is no more nor no less illusory than society. It would seem to be less so. It seems to me to be a more complete self-evident truth.

: : :

I am rather inclined to think that it is the Self that exists rather than all the rest. It would appear at present that it is the rest that exists. The rest: society, the structural form of groups. Groups, however, do not have a consciousness of their own. Groups obey rules. They are determined. Might they not be determined by another consciousness? This consciousness may transcend them. A consciousness, or, if I may so put it, a spirit or the determining spirit beyond or behind groups. Could this not justify both individualism and (*pace* sociology) metaphysics?

: : :

Everything within me is in motion: passions, drives, and impulses. This is not my Self. This is within me. I am not what is put in motion. I am what puts in motion. I am also the one that allows himself to be put in motion. But I am set in motion in my own way, which is like no other. Everyone allows himself to be acted upon in a different way.

: : :

I am determined. At the same time, I also determine. I make a choice, I fail to make a choice, I change or I do not change things, and the fact that I do not change things causes them to change all the same. My way of determining is also determined. The universe can be considered to be a group or whole of events that determine each other reciprocally and thus participate in the universal energy and universal purposes. I am a particularization of the universal soul, of the universal consciousness. Einstein thought, in all seriousness, that he could see purposes in the dynamics of the Manifestation. As a matter of fact, when one discovers fundamental structural laws, one is perhaps only recognizing the existence, the reality in particular wholes of a universal determining principle of these particular wholes of creation, partaking of the universal soul to the degree that it is manifested, participating in what this soul possesses that manifests itself, in what it possesses that causes it to desire to appear. The

universal soul or the *atman*. One has the impression
that little by little we are coming round to discovering
the underlying laws of a universal guiding principle.
But the particular Self, the individual soul, which is
like a whirlpool in the river's flow, cannot fail to be
very important, since it exists. Neither more nor less
determined than collective groupings, *I* exist just as
much as the rest; illusion is reality itself.

: : :

By comparison to what is happening at present in
the modern world of ideas—structuralism, the philosophy of science, which are profoundly antihumanist—
both existentialism and Marxism seem to me to be
luminously humanistic. Marxism in the last analysis
is an ethic and a religion, or a metaphysic, or a my-
thology. To proclaim that one is trying to prevent the
exploitation of man by man, that it is "evil" to so exploit man, is a moral thought. It is even a petit-bourgeois ethic; it is even a Christian ethic. That is to say:
a Jewish ethic.

Moreover, if one wanted to "demystify," as the expression goes today, or rather to shed light on what is
at the bottom of the different sorts of socialism, one
would rediscover all the myths of the Old and New
Testament: the Ideal City, the New Jerusalem, Paradise Lost, the going beyond History, and the essential
myth, the upward march, the "technique" of redemption: progress. How can anyone believe in progress
without being a mystic? Why should there be progress?
This is really the myth par excellence of the Upward
Way.

: : :

Everybody wants to lead everybody else. Everybody opposes being led by everybody else. This establishes an equilibrium that is at least dynamic. (*1940.*)

: : :

1967: The "conflict" in the Middle East has quieted down somewhat. It has prevented me from busying myself with literature for three or four weeks. Now I can go back to it again. From time to time we are plunged into the midst of events. Then a precarious calm is restored. We fall back into illusion. Then we can coin fine literary phrases and speak, for example, of the fact that we know that the precarious calm of this moment is illusory. We are aware of it, and yet not aware of it at all. We speak of illusion and of what is not illusion. We are in the midst of illusion and still have one foot in reality. If I say: "How I should like for there to be peace, how I should like to love this world that I love but love it even more, how I should like to love," people answer me, it's because you want to be loved, but there is nothing to love, love is a deceptive myth. That is doubtless true. Loving is perhaps a sort of cowardice: it is wanting to be defended, because those who love you are your defenders, and not wanting to fight. Of course. But I can reply that hatred is not any less stupid than love and that wanting to fight corresponds to ancestral reflexes and that that too has to be "demystified." One mustn't love, one mustn't hate; but one must also not fail to love or fail to hate. During the other conflicts, the other wars, revolutions, and upheavals that I have gone through in my life, all I have ever really done is to live through them. How to wage war alongside the Germans? How to make war alongside the Russians who took half of the Moldavian provinces that belonged to the Romanians, for at that time I was a Romanian. And how to wage war to defend Romania, that country that I didn't like, that country in which I felt so uncomfortable that I didn't feel that it was mine. I got out. Believing that it was absurd and that they were stupid to fight, I was proud of not "going along" and of sneaking out, thanks to my situation that allowed me to be neither Romanian nor French, or sometimes one and sometimes the other, whichever was to my advantage. This was a cynicism full of vitality, a youthful cynicism. And I rebelled.

Then it became more and more impossible for me to be indifferent. If millions and millions of people die, that is tolerable. But if they are massacred by other men, it is no longer tolerable. My revolt was, and remains, romantic. Luckily. It is not political, for anyone who takes sides is a killer in any event. It is the human condition that I find intolerable. It is being on this earth that is intolerable. It is not being able to understand that is intolerable, and we cannot understand because finitude is our distinguishing characteristic. I continue to be naive as I rebel, as once I was candid in my cynicism, but I now can no longer bear for civilizations to disappear, for nations to fall to pieces, for societies to be broken up and dispersed, for universes to burst into flame and collapse.

I am obviously on Israel's side. Perhaps because I have read the Bible. Perhaps because my education was Christian and because after all Christianity is only a Jewish sect. Perhaps because, if I was able to bear the death of five or ten or fifteen or twenty million persons, I can no longer bear the death of twenty million and one persons: as the saying goes, this would be the straw that would break the camel's back. I know too that the Jews made their fallow land fertile. I know that their neighbors cannot do so and are jealous. I know that the progressivist Arab states are not progressivist and that military and Fascist castes are leading them in Egypt and Algeria. In short, I am for the Jews. In the end I have chosen this people, even if this people is only a little less bad than the others. I know too that the leaders of Algeria live on hatred, on mad pretentions to grandeur: the imperialist Nasser, the killer of Yemenites and Sudanese.

When hostilities broke out, when people believed that everything was lost for Israel, I despairingly asked an Israeli diplomat what I could do. "Even if it's only writing an article in some newspaper," I said. "That's a lot," he answered. "Do it; everything counts."

I wrote this article; I published it. I wrote another. And I had the feeling that I had really done something. Something useful, a very small thing, but nonetheless I felt that I had done this small thing conscientiously, that I had not been completely useless. I had the impression that I had been something like a noncommissioned officer during the war who's done his little task with his little platoon, or that I had been one of the voices, one of the hundreds of thousands of voices that cause the balance to weigh heavier on the side of an elect.

: : :

I go back to these papers at the beginning of the other war: I find this. No one has the right to possess the world. No one fails to try to do so. (I have not really changed my mind.)

1941: . . . If we lived in another time, a time without terror and anguish, I would be tortured by boredom, the sadness of existing, the ambitions of a career. I would like to overcome this fury and this terror; I cannot. In days gone by I had work to do, and laziness prevented me from doing it. At any event, whatever the circumstances, I experience the same inability to surpass myself in one way or another. Laziness and fury—that is to say, the symptoms of impossibility.

: : :

General ideas, too general ideas. Very general ideas. Ideas not very general. Ideas not general enough. Ideas of the general. Ideas of the general's wife, the generous general's wife. The general ideas of the generous general's wife. Generally, the general ideas of the general's wife are generous. The generals, generously invited to the general dress rehearsal. Generals of the young generation. Generating generals. In general, one can call it the generation of generals. Genetics. Gehenna. Relegating the generous general of the young generation to Gehenna. Let us regenerate our generals. A regenerated general. A jejune engendering general. This regenerated general of the jejune generation is becoming a general bore. The generalities of the prolonged genetics lecture generally bored the generous young general. Generous general, a noble horse? Don't bother, ingeniously generous generals. Generally the generous young general of the jejune generation went to Genoa to regenerate his geniality and generalize his ideas, his chromosomes, and their generative genes. General generosity. Generals generally ingenious about generalities. General generosity, generated by genes. General generosity, general generosity, generous generation.

: : :

I meet L. A great writer and a great critic. Too great a writer and too great a critic. I can think of nothing but the war, of course, since it is wartime. I see him coming toward me. He holds out his hand to me. He is radiant. There has just been a public celebration of his sixtieth birthday. A review devoted an entire issue to him, around three hundred pages. "Have you read this review?" he asks me.

None of this interested me at all. Literature is for vacations. There are so few vacations. In fact, there aren't any at all. Yet people take them from time to time anyway. I take practically none. My mind is too occupied. Perhaps this is an error. Perhaps I am mistaken. Perhaps it merely seems to me that there is war, misfortune, death. At this moment especially I have the strong impression that there is a war. So I haven't read the review L. was talking to me about. Could I be so impolite as to answer: "The war and the fate of the world prevent me from thinking of anything else; and even if there were no war my own anxiety concerns me much more than your Prodigious Personality"?

"Certainly, sir, certainly. They've written very nice things about you, my hearty congratulations. Moreover, I myself intended to . . ." Then I tried to change the subject.

"Well, then, tell me," he persisted, "which article did you like the best?"

I knew that V. had written an article on L. I said:

"I liked V.'s article best."

"That's not my opinion," L. replied. "The warmest, most animated article, the one that touched me the most was S.'s. Of course, V. did paint a very good portrait of me. It was flattering and admiring, but S. not only showed his admiration for me, he also showed such affection that really . . ."

And L. continued in this vein all the way along the boulevard till we reached his house. I am his neighbor.

: : :

The war in the Pacific. The first battles in the air and on the sea were victories for the Japanese. They are going to occupy Indonesia. They are going to occupy Australia, they are going to occupy New Zealand. What in the world are the Americans doing? Their bases were attacked and most of them were won in a few hours; their battleships and cruisers were destroyed. The press, following Hitler's line, says: "The Americans have no business in the Pacific; what are they doing so far from home?"

: : :

Sensational events in the Pacific. American ships continue to be sunk; Japanese troops are taking over all the islands. The Americans were not prepared for war. Their garrisons and armaments in the Philippines and Havana were ridiculously small. The Japanese are armed to the teeth. The Japanese soldiers themselves turn into human torpedoes . . . The English battleships have been sunk. The English and the Americans will soon be without a navy. Who will save France, who will save us?

: : :

June 1967: It's war in the Middle East. Heroism and nobility on the part of the Israelis. I am obliged to use these words because they mean what they say. The hateful world of the Pan-Arab movement.

What can I do? I have written an article on Israel. I have sent telegrams. And I have signed a manifesto.

And then I have kept on writing and writing. This activity—my activity—seems more obviously vain to me than usual. There is one blinding truth about war, stupidity, courage, ignominy: the truth of death. And this truth goes beyond what has made it such a blinding truth: appetites, pride, political and ideological.

The blinding light of truth, a light that reveals the lack of importance of anything else, is there in the war, and no longer has any relationship to the reasons for this war and the causes of this war.

Despite wars, however, despite revolutions, despite natural catastrophes, despite invasions, despite the centuries, despite the changes of societies and of languages and ways of thinking, texts may still exist to bear witness to death but also to life. The memoirs of a Japanese lady at court in the eleventh century, the memoirs of a bourgeois of the sixteenth century have come down to us through innumerable disasters. It is necessary to leave traces.

Around 1940: I am sick of the white race.

One ought to be totally indifferent to history, men, their histories. This is nót possible. My angry temperament is both anxiety-ridden and stronger than everything else. Too many fits of anger, too much pity, too much fear. To think that I might have been the most ironic person in the universe. Too bad to have made a bad job of all that.

: : :

1967 or 1966: In any case, here are some recent pages that seem so much like those I wrote more than twenty years ago that I must add them to the earlier ones; if only I could manage not to be irritated, not to get angry, not to let myself be carried away! First of all, I would argue matters better, I would explain myself better. It's very odd: I am less of a dupe than almost anyone else; I don't let myself be blindly taken in by clichés, abstract systems, cleverness, ideological hypocrisy, consciously or unconsciously hypocritical ideology or the current of opinion, but I am still blinded when I realize how blinded other people are; I am blinded, I have blurred vision. But in order to explain the misplaced grudges of writers "in revolt," in order to explain what underlies their behavior, it is necessary to be detached, to be free as regards one's own person, not to be carried away by one's hatred at the way other people are carried away, which results in one's being more carried away than those who are carried away.

: : :

Blind people think they can see. Parakeets imagine that they can think. Fashionable progressivists of the world don't know that they might just as well have been fashionable members of Action Française in 1935

. . . (But I interrupt the transcription of this diatribe. I notice that it is directed against the host of followers of Sartre. But today Sartre no longer has any followers. The new philosophers know very well what is happening: today there is a desperate struggle to re-evaluate Marxism. Others believe that Marxism has been superseded. But in any case those with superior minds are perfectly aware that Marxism has failed socially, or rather that the Russian temperament, the Russian nature has won out over socialism.)

: : :

Around 1940: Whatever happens, war, upheavals, revolutions, or whatever, I take those who in the chaos of history and despite everything that politics and events do to monopolize, to absorb the thought of men, do not allow themselves to be entirely monopolized by politics and economics, those who in periods of order or anarchy never console themselves for the fact that they cannot decipher the divine enigma, those who do not lose sight of the problem of the ultimate purposes of the universe, to be an elite. Willy-nilly, I am part of the world. This makes me inconsolable.

: : :

Fatigue. Fatigue. At the end of my rope. Helplessness. I have a few ideas. Impossible to string them together. I would like to put the universe in order. I am amazed that I cannot do so all by myself. No one will listen to me. Not everyone has the same ideas. Imagine: it is impossible for me to command the obedience of two billion persons. Everyone, or almost everyone, is tempted to command the obedience of everyone. This brings on the appearance of dictators. There are also antidictators. If there were only one dictator in the whole world this might be all right. (*1967:*

People today ought to accord de Gaulle full power over the
whole universe; we'd at least have a good laugh.)

: : :

1941: Here are some catchwords that are making the
rounds: "It is better to be the servants of the Germans than
the slaves of the Yids." "Of course, the Germans have occupied the country. They are not friends. But at least they
avenge us for being occupied by others, the Jews." (*1967:*
The British and the Americans were as hated by the ex-
tremists and the French of the left as they are today by
others.)

: : :

We could understand everything that is happening if only
we were not troubled by exaggerated feelings. It is fearing
for our own persons and our own personal interests that
keeps us from seeing things clearly. It is being committed
that keeps one from dominating the situation. This is obvious. We ought to keep telling ourselves this.

: : :

It is as if there were two human races: Man and New
Man.

The New Man seems to me to be different from Man
not only psychologically but physically. I am not a New
Man. I am a Man. Imagine that one fine morning you discover that rhinoceroses have taken power. They have a
rhinoceros ethics, a rhinoceros philosophy, a rhinoceros
universe. The new master of the city is a rhinoceros who
uses the same words as you and yet it is not the same language. The words have a different meaning for him. How
can we ever understand each other? (*No. In fact, rhinoc-*
eroses have deliberately distorted, deliberately diverted the
meaning of words, which is the same for them, which they
understand but which they corrupted for propaganda pur-
poses. It is not a new sort of thought, not a new language,

but a clever manipulation of terms so as to create confusion in the minds of their adversaries, or to get those who are undecided on their side.)

Second Tale for Children Less Than Three Years Old

This morning, as usual, Josette knocks at the door of her parents' bedroom. Daddy hasn't slept very well. Mama has gone to the country for a few days. So daddy has taken advantage of her being gone to eat lots of sausages, to drink beer, to eat pork pâté, and many other things that mama won't let him eat because it's not good for his health. So now daddy has a pain in his liver, a stomach-ache, a headache, and would prefer not to be waked up. But Josette is still knocking at the door. So daddy tells her to come in. She comes in and goes over to her daddy. Mama is gone. Josette asks:

"Where's mama?"

Daddy answers: "Your mama's gone to the country to her mama's for a rest."

Josette answers: "To granny's?"

Daddy replies: "Yes, to granny's."

"Write mama," Josette says. "Telephone mama," Josette says.

Daddy says: "We mustn't telephone." And then daddy says to himself: "Because maybe she's somewhere else . . ."

Josette says: "Tell me a story with you and mama and me in it."

"No," daddy says, "I'm going to work. I'm going to get up and get dressed."

And daddy gets up. He puts his red bathrobe on over his pajamas, he puts his "slipperies" on, and goes to the bathroom. He closes the bathroom door. Josette is at the bathroom door. She knocks with her little fists, she cries.

Josette says: "Open the door."

Daddy says: "I can't, I'm stark naked, I'm washing, and then I'm going to shave."

Josette says: "And you're doing number one and number two."

"I'm washing," daddy says.

Josette says: "You're washing your face, you're washing your shoulders, you're washing your arms, you're washing your back, you're washing your bottom, you're washing your feet."

"I'm shaving my beard," daddy says.

"You're shaving your beard with soap," Josette says. "I want to come in and see."

Daddy says: "You can't see me, because I'm not in the bathroom anymore."

Josette says (behind the door): "Well, where are you then?"

Daddy answers: "I don't know. Go and see. Maybe I'm in the dining room. Go look for me."

Josette runs into the dining room and daddy begins washing. Josette runs into the dining room on her short little legs. Daddy has peace and quiet, but not for long. Josette comes back to the door of the bathroom and laughs through the door.

Josette says: "I looked for you. You aren't in the dining room."

Daddy says: "You didn't look well enough. Go look under the table."

Josette goes into the dining room again, then comes back. She says: "You aren't under the table."

Daddy says: "Well, then, go look in the living room. Look carefully and see whether I'm in the chair, on the couch, behind the books, at the window."

Josette goes away. Daddy has peace and quiet, but not for long.

Josette comes back.

She says: "No, you're not in the chair, you're not at the window, you're not on the couch, you're not behind the books, you're not in the television set, you're not in the living room."

Daddy says: "Well, then, go and see if I'm in the kitchen."

Josette says: "I'm going to go look for you in the kitchen."

Josette runs into the kitchen. Daddy has peace and quiet, but not for long.

Josette comes back.

She says: "You aren't in the kitchen."

Daddy says: "Take a good look under the kitchen table, look and see if I'm in the buffet, look and see if I'm in the pans, look and see if I'm in the oven with the chicken."

Josette goes off and then comes back. Daddy isn't in the oven, daddy isn't in the pans, daddy isn't in the buffet, daddy isn't under the mattress, daddy isn't in the pocket of his pants, the only thing in the pocket of his pants is a handkerchief.

Josette comes back to the door of the bathroom.

Josette says: "I've looked everywhere, but I can't find you. Where are you?"

Daddy says: "I'm here." And daddy, who's had time to get washed and shaved and dressed, opens the door.

He says: "Here I am." He takes Josette in his arms, and just then the front door opens and there's mama. Josette jumps down out of her daddy's arms and throws herself in her mama's arms. She kisses her and says:

"Mama, I looked for daddy under the table, in the closet, under the rug, behind the mirror, in the kitchen, and in the garbage can, but he wasn't there."

Daddy says to mama: "I'm glad you're back. Was it nice in the country? How's your mother?"

Josette says: "How's granny? Are we going to her house?"

III

1967: Friendship between men has long since disappeared. Did it ever exist? When people draw up petitions, when they demonstrate for the poor children in Vietnam, they don't think for a moment about the population of entire villages of Yemenites showered with napalm or burned out by the Egyptians. The misfortunes of the Vietnamese people don't interest them. What interests them is making anti-American propaganda. When people speak of the unfortunate Cubans during the rule of Batista, they don't give a moment's thought to the hundreds of thousands of Cubans who have fled Castro and emigrated. "I saw two or three of them in a plane," my friend M. says to me. "They're no good to anyone, they don't understand a thing, they must be all alike. It's only the old people who are fleeing." When people speak of the destruction of the Tibetan state, and pity the population that has fled or been massacred, they only talk about it if they detest Mao.

Not long ago there was an international congress on theater. D., who is now a Communist after having been a Fascist, long ago of course, said that dramatists were not doing their duty because they weren't writing plays about famine in India. Someone in the audience got to his feet and said that those who were starving in India didn't need plays but shipments of bread. D. turned red with anger: it wasn't bread they really needed, according to him, but rather to be fed pro-Communist propaganda. Peter Weiss wrote a whole play on the Nazi executioners put on trial at Nuremberg; at the moment when the Egyptians were preparing to massacre the Jews, and saying so, stating so, talking of a holy war, and being seen and heard doing so by all the humanists in the West, Peter Weiss made no public protest against the genocide that was being planned, that still is being planned against Israel.

There is something that troubles me even more: Hochhuth wrote a famous play against Pope Pius XII, whom he accused not of being pro-Nazi, but of being anti-Nazi in too cowardly, too wishy-washy a way, and of not having protested against the murder of the Jews. There is something more curious still: at the moment when Paul VI was attempting to reconcile all parties with Israel, at the moment when he was trying to calm people, not a word from Hochhuth appeared in the press. Hochhuth, however, did something else: he wrote a play against Churchill who, for his part, at least, could not be accused of not having done his best to defeat Nazism . . . His attitude seems to me to be revealing. A few days before the war in the Middle East, there were many names among the signatories of the German manifestoes against the genocide of Israel that was being planned. But neither the name of Peter Weiss nor that of Hochhuth appeared on any of them.

But has there been any protest against the mass murder of the Sudanese in the south, black or Christian, by Egyptian Moslems? This "populace" was really of no interest to anyone. When the French and the Algerians were killing each other, when Algerians were killing other Algerians, the "democratic" press was full of humanitarian protests against the tortures inflicted on the Algerians by the French. There was a great deal of talk about the case of Alleg, who was tortured by the French police. But not a word was said about his book when he began to write about the way the Algerian police behaved. Immediately after the Algerian war there was one of the worst earthquakes ever in Morocco. Not everyone could be rescued. Hundreds of dead and hundreds still living were buried under the ruins that the authorities covered over with bulldozers in order to prevent a possible epidemic. No one has said anything about these innocent dead. What was there to say, since the Algerian war was over? On the cover of *L'Express* was a photograph of Zazie. "Up yours," she was saying. Yes, "up yours" to all the corpses that are of no interest to me politically: what can I do?

But if, on the other hand, someone sees a cat run over in the street or if the police stop you from overfeeding the pigeons that spread some disease or other, what a howl is raised by sensitive souls! When the American astronauts were burned alive in the cabin of their spacecraft, people were not nearly as touched, of course, because they were Americans, as when a Russian astronaut suffered the same fate, and infinitely less touched than when a female cat or a monkey was shot into space before men were. On these latter occasions there were long lines of demonstrators in London in front of the U.S. and Russian embassies.

Is this because animals are innocent and good and men cruel and wicked? Not at all. Animals are cruel. In fact, they are ferocious. I believe, however, that no animal species hates itself as much as we do.

: : :

There are facts that people refuse to realize. In Greece, the new extreme-right regime not only imposes censorship and puts people in prison; it also causes "spontaneously indignant" passers-by to slash miniskirts in the street and takes men with beards to a barbershop by force. This makes people in the West indignant; in the countries in the Eastern bloc "spontaneously indignant" passers-by also slash miniskirts and shave men with beards. It's no use to mention this to people who have just shown how indignant they were at the excesses or the instances of brutality on the part of the Greek authorities. The same brutality in the countries in the Eastern bloc hasn't had any effect on them; they have not reacted. Socialist beard-wearers, however, had logic on their side. They said: "Listen, Marx had a beard; Castro has a beard." "Yes!" the police answered, never being at a loss in an argument, "but they wore beards in a society that was illegal. Since the old illegality has become legal, beards are no longer legal." There is other, more serious testimony. Let us say no more of all the people who flee, who are killed trying to get over the Berlin wall. But does anybody pay attention to Ginzburg's book on the Soviet death camps, which existed not only under Stalin but still exist, since Sinyavsky and Daniel are locked up in them, or to Stalin's daughter's

escape and the story she has told? And will what I
say myself be heard? As a matter of fact, I realize
how ridiculous and naive I am being. Everybody knows
the things that I'm saying. And they say nothing about
what they know because that's what they want. What's
needed is for everything to go badly. If only humanity
could be destroyed faster: that's what people want.

For centuries humanity lived either amid tyranny or
amid disorder. I prefer disorder to tyranny. The Revolution managed to combine disorder and tyranny.

: : :

The world is led by mad leaders. The Russian leaders, for example. France is led by a general who now
has but one pleasure: doing whatever he feels like
even if it's not a good thing. In China there is Mao's
paranoia, the mad folly of a bloody island that is
transmitted to dazed hordes who are ready for anything. China proclaims that it prefers the destruction
of the world to a European or an American peace. Let
the whole world perish, China included, if China
doesn't manage to dominate the whole world: this is
exactly what Hitler said of Germany.

When China is ready to wage atomic war, the attack against humanity will be immediately unleashed.

: : :

The blindness of people in the West was a painful
surprise to me. But this no longer astonishes me; it
frightens me, ever since I have realized, ever since I
have been aware that the "blindness" is deliberate.
Sartre is not alone, for example, in his pigheadedness.
He reflects the mentality of the petit bourgeois whose

feelings have been corrupted and whose minds, of course, have been corrupted too. The petit bourgeois who is a "revolutionary," out of self-hatred and out of hatred for others who are petit bourgeois. Out of fear of revolutionaries as well. Blindness, deceit, bad faith. French intellectuals of this sort are hated and scorned by all really progressivist intellectuals in the East where tyranny reigns.

: : :

A few months ago I met an Anglo-Irish journalist, a refined, mediocre, shortsighted man who turned out to have no notion of anything. He spoke to me of the "power madness" rampant in the world. I thought I had met somebody who agreed with me. I thought he was going to talk to me about Russia, about Nasser, about the struggle of Arab leaders for power, about Mao. Not at all: he talked to me about the tyranny that reigns in England or in France, of the persecutions in these countries. He didn't even mention Portugal.

: : :

I have never known any poor Communists. I have known many rich Communists: artists, theatrical directors, rich producers, bourgeois of the sixteenth arrondissement in Paris, and even a few millionaires. A way of being protected from all sides, no matter what happens.

: : :

It's quite true. It's exactly as the old Jews said it was: man is wicked by nature. We don't like ourselves. That's what it is. Otherwise matters could be easily arranged, no one would exploit anyone, we would all make concessions to each other, everybody

would like serving everybody else, there would be
neither servants nor masters, people would cooperate;
but it so happens that there are only masters who are
scornful of their servants, servants detesting their masters, and no social organization has ever changed this
state of affairs in the slightest. The man who loves
others is mad. The supreme hypocrisy is that people
don't want to admit that this is true. Hypocrisy consists
of excuses, the smile of humanism; hypocrisy consists
of all this being done in the name of justice. People
no longer dare to say: all this is being done in the
name of charity.

: : :

There will be no more day. There will be no more
night. There will be no more dawn. There will be no
more twilight. There will be no more time. There will
be no more space.

And that little being that I saw suffering, that I saw
faint, that I saw love, will be no more. This saddens
me more than the destruction of everything.

: : :

Around 1940: The police are rhinoceroses. The judges
are rhinoceroses. You are the only man among the rhinoceroses. The rhinoceroses wonder how the world could
have been led by men. You yourself wonder: is it true that
the world was led by men?

What can be done to win France back? One can still
make oneself understood on this issue at least. You have
the impression in the end that this very desire is a guilty
one. It is something of a sin not to be a rhinoceros. But
rhinoceroses fight each other. Hundreds of thousands of

rhinoceroses pour in from the north, from the east, from the west. All armies are armies of rhinoceroses. All soldiers of just causes are rhinoceroses. All holy wars are the doing of rhinoceroses. Justice is the doing of rhinoceroses. Revolutions are the doing of rhinoceroses.

—It is as if I found myself in another time and space. Another planet.

—Here is a rhinoceros slogan, a slogan of the "New Man" that a man can't understand: everything for the State, everything for the Nation, everything for the Race. This seems monstrous to me, obviously. What I will admit is this: everything for God, if one is a believer; or, if not, everything for man, for men, for the joy of man, for the perfecting of man. How can anyone be for the State, which is only an administrative machine? It is not a man, it is not God, it is not an angel, it is not even an idea, a myth. It is an abstraction, or rather it is a justice-machine, but for rhinoceroses the State has become a God. How is that possible? What can they have put into this void, what can they have filled it up with, what can they have projected into it? People didn't have any use for God, because God alienates you, and then all of a sudden they have made the State a God in order to be alienated. You could speak with God personally, *whether He existed or not.* You spoke to Him and He answered—or at least you believed that He answered. He was chased away. The Messiah was behind the door. But no one would open it. But above all it was this personal reality, a true one or an imaginary one, of the existence of God that was essential, living, comforting. But if God is only myself, even if He is only my projection, even if when I speak to Him it is as if I were speaking to myself in front of my mirror, this gives me a concrete image; it does not alienate but rather affirms or confirms my existence, my personality. But what is the State, how can one project oneself into the State, and what is the Nation, and what is Society? Abstractions, depersonalizing ones, not existential ones, stinking ones, supremely alienating ones. Humanity does not exist. There are men. Society does not exist. There are friends. It is not the same thing for a rhinoceros. For me, his State is a phantom. For him, it is the concrete person who is a phantom. (*1967: When I wrote this, I was talking about the Fascist mentality and the Iron Guards and their collectivism. Today this would apply to Marxists and Marxist societies.*)

The New Man can live in the impersonal. He has given up his person. God can be conceived only as a person. Men are persons. If one gives oneself to the Nation, if the Nation, Society are God, there is no one left.

: : :

I was chatting with S. We were talking quietly. Then we discussed politics. He is anti-Nazi of course, and anti-Iron Guard. Nonetheless he says: "The Iron Guards are not right. They are not right on all points. However, you must admit—and you know I'm not an anti-Semite—you must admit that the Jews too . . ." etc. "You know that I am against the Iron Guards. However, they call for moral and spiritual values which . . ." I rise to my feet in terror. This is the way they all begin. They admit certain things, with complete objectivity. You must discuss things with them reasonably and objectively. In reality they give in a little, to the right, to the left, without realizing it. They make concessions. They don't realize it. In reality, they stick their fingers in the machinery. They will soon be swallowed up by Moloch. If one admits a single one of their postulates one ends up admitting them all. It is inevitable. I know what's involved. All my anti-Fascist friends have become absolute, fanatic Fascists because in the beginning they gave in on one little detail. I am well acquainted with this phenomenon: the incubation period has begun; these are the first symptoms. It takes them between three weeks and two months to become part of the system. They all begin like that. Sometimes they don't even have to open their mouths for me to realize that they've changed. A silence full of meaning, a smile, make me realize that something irremediable has happened. That they've been caught. The expression on their faces changes. There's a certain light in their eyes. They all have an excuse: purity. But what is there behind this purity? Purity is a hoax. (*Today, in 1967, we would say that purity is a "myth," and that this myth ought to be "demystified."*)

: : :

I spoke to him. He was still a man. Suddenly, beneath my very eyes, I saw his skin get hard and thicken in a terrifying way. His gloves, his shoes, became hoofs; his hands became paws, a horn began to grow out of his forehead, he became ferocious, he attacked furiously. He was no longer intelligent, he could no longer talk. He had become a rhinoceros. I would like very much to follow his example. But I can't.

: : :

I cannot live without the presence of beauty. Everything is ugly in this country; everything seems cheap and common to me. I think of certain hillsides in France, of the city of Paris, of oceans. The beauty of the Tuileries, and then of the mountains. And then the rivers, and then the poplars, and then the cathedrals . . .

: : :

When one has been unlucky enough to be born, one should at least have the consolation of living well, of living comfortably. If one lives badly, one has been duped twice over. I am the victim of a bad joke: who played it? If one is so unfortunate as to be alive, if one is conscious of being alive, one ought at least not to be afraid of death. The most absurd thing is to be conscious of the fact that human existence is unbearable, that the human condition is unbearable, intolerable, and nonetheless cling desperately to it, knowing and complaining that one is going to lose what is unbearable. Like someone who is being hanged, who wants the rope to be cut and does not want it to be cut, because underneath there is a stake.

Torn to pieces between the horror of living and the horror of dying.

: : :

M. has just married a young girl, a very beautful, very pure one, it would appear. She cheated on him three weeks before the wedding. She told him so. He had noticed that something serious, something mysterious had happened and she finally confessed. She told him how it had happened. She was simply walking in the street, a man accosted her, and she immediately followed him to a hotel. She experienced pleasure, she said. He is furious and very upset. He is sick over it. He sends her away, takes her back, forgives her. But he does not forget. She has never seen the other man again. But the young husband thinks of this adventure day and night; he cannot contain his jealousy. He is so jealous that he envies the other man. How lucky he was, he says. He would like to be in the other man's place, to experience the happiness, the joy of being followed by his own wife. But that is not enough: in order for it to bring him even greater joy, someone must suffer because of it. Someone else must be mortally jealous. Stealing his wife from someone is his fondest dream.

: : :

It is very simple. The world must be led by those interested in leading it. Who deserves to lead the world? Those whom it interests, those who want to bother with it. Let them conquer the world. This doesn't interest me.

: : :

How long, how much longer is all this going to last?

: : :

The last day of the year 1941. Last year, on the night of the thirty-first of December, I made an appointment with myself on this day and this night. I hoped that everything would be over. I promise to meet myself next year. I hope that we will still be alive. Last year, I hoped that I would be able to leave the country again. I now have the impression that I am completely paralyzed, that I cannot move a muscle. But I'll soon be myself again. I have sources of energy; I have endless will power and am extremely stubborn. I will do anything to get out of this country. I give myself an appointment for next year. I will no longer be here.

Third Tale for Children Less Than Three Years Old

One morning little Josette knocks at the door of her parents' bedroom to wake them up, as she had the day before and as she had every morning. Her mama was already awake; she was up out of bed and already taking her bath. She had gone to bed early and had slept well. Her daddy was still sleeping because he had gone to a restaurant, and then to the movies, and then back to the restaurant, and then to a puppet show, and then back to the restaurant, all alone. And now he wanted to sleep because he said it was Sunday, and because on Sunday daddies don't have to go to work and don't have to go get the car to go to the country either because it's winter and there is ice all over the roads.

There's ice on the roads. The radio said so. But there's no ice in Paris. In Paris it's quite a nice day. There are a few clouds above the houses, but there is also a blue sky above the trees on the avenue.

Josette walks along next to her daddy; she tickles his nose; daddy makes a face and she kisses him; daddy thinks it's a little dog. It's not a little dog; it's his little girl.

"Tell me a story," Josette says to her daddy.

So daddy begins a story.

"A story about you and me," Josette says.

And daddy tells a story about Josette and her daddy.

Here is daddy's story. He says to Josette: "We're going to have a ride in an airplane. I'm going to put your socks on you, and your panties, your little skirt, your flannel undervest, your little pink sweater."

Josette: "No, not that one."

Daddy: "Well, then, this one, the white one."

Josette: "Yes, the white one."

Daddy: "I'm going to put your white sweater on you. Then I'm going to put your little coat, your little gloves on you. Oh, I've forgotten your boots. I'm going to put your little hat on you. I'm going to get out of bed, get dressed, and take you by the hand. You'll see. We're going to knock on the bathroom door. Mama will say: 'Where are you going, dears?' "

Josette: "I'm going for a ride in an airplane with daddy."

"Mama will say: 'Have a good time, dears. Be good, be careful. If you're going in an airplane, you have to see to it that Josette doesn't lean out the window. It's dangerous. She might fall in the Seine or on the neighbor lady's roof and hurt her little bottom or get a big bump on her forehead.'

"Daddy says: 'Goodbye, mama.' "

Josette says: "Goodbye, mama."

Daddy says: "We're going to go to the end of the corridor, and then turn to the right. The corridor isn't dark there. It gets light through the windows of the living room on the left. Then we'll come to the kitchen where Jacqueline is fixing lunch. We'll say to her: 'Goodbye, Jacqueline.' "

Josette: "Goodbye, Jacqueline."

"Jacqueline will say: 'Where are you going, sir? Where are you going with your daddy, Josette?' "

Josette: "We're going for a ride. We're going to go up in an airplane. We're going up into the sky."

"Jacqueline will say: 'Watch Josette when you get up there, sir. She mustn't lean out the window. It's dangerous. She might fall. She might get a bump on her forehead if she falls on the neighbor's roof. Or she might get caught in the branches of a tree by the bottom of her panties. We'd have to go get her with a ladder.' "

Josette: "No, I'll be very careful."

"Then," daddy says, "I'll take the key and open the door."

Josette: "You'll put the key in the keyhole."

Daddy: "I open the door, I close the door, I don't slam the door, I close the door gently, I get in the elevator with you, I press the button . . ."

Josette: "No, I'll press the button. Take me in your arms because I'm too little."

Daddy: "I take you in my arms. You press the button. The elevator goes down so it can go up later on. We go down to the ground floor. We get out of the elevator. There's the concierge outside her office sweeping."

Josette: "Good morning, madame."

Daddy: "And then the concierge says: 'Good morning, sir, good morning, darling. Oh, how pretty she is this morning, with her pretty little coat, her pretty little shoes, her pretty little gloves, oh, what little hands she has . . .' "

Josette: "And my hat . . ."

"The concierge says: 'Where are you going all dressed up like that? Are you going for a walk?' "

Josette: "For a ride in an airplane."

Daddy: "Then the concierge says to us: 'You must be careful. You mustn't let your little girl lean out of the window of the airplane, sir, because she might fall . . .' "

Josette: "And hurt my little bottom on the neighbor's roof or get a big bump on my forehead . . ."

Daddy: "Or on your nose. So then the concierge says to us: 'Have a good time.' We go out onto the street. We meet Michou's mama and go by the butcher shop with the calves' heads."

Josette (hiding her eyes): "I don't want to look. Bad butcher."

Daddy: "Yes, if the butcher kills any more calves I'm going to kill the butcher. We reach the corner of the street, we go across the street, be careful of the cars. We go across another street and come to the bus stop. Here's the bus; we take it."

Josette: "It stops and goes, stops and goes . . ."

Daddy: "And here we are at the airport. We take the airplane and it goes up and up. Like my hand . . . vrrr . . . vrrr . . ."

Josette: "It goes up and up, vrrr . . . vrrr . . ."

Daddy: "We look through the window."

Josette: "We mustn't lean out."

Daddy: "Don't be afraid, I'm holding you. See the streets down there. There's our house. You can see the neighbor's house."

Josette: "I don't want to fall on his roof . . ."

Daddy: "You can see the street, the cars down there; they're all very small; you can see the people in the streets; they're very small; you can see the Porte de Saint-Cloud, the Bois de Vincennes, the zoo with the animals."

Josette: "Hello there, animals."

Daddy: "See the lion; listen—he's going grrr . . . grrr . . ." and daddy shows what the lion does with his claws and growls fiercely: "Grrr . . ."

Josette: "No, don't do that; you aren't a lion, are you? You're a daddy . . . You're not a lion."

Daddy: "No, I'm not a lion. I'm a daddy. I was just pretending, to show you."

Josette: "No, don't do it anymore."

Daddy: "And then the airplane goes up and up . . ."

Josette: "It goes up and up and up . . ."

Daddy: "And you can see the countryside."

Josette: "Mills . . ."

Daddy: "Yes, you can see the mill at La Chapelle-Anthenaise and Marie in the farmyard . . ."

Josette: "The ducks . . ."

Daddy: "The river . . ."

Josette: "The fish swimming in the water; you mustn't eat the fish."

Daddy: "No, you don't eat nice fish, only bad fish. The bad fish eat the nice fish. So you have to eat the bad fish."

Josette: "Not the nice fish."

Daddy: "No, not the nice ones, only the bad ones. And then you can see Papa Robert, and the meadows, and Papa Robert's little girl."

Josette: "She's a bad girl; she got my dress dirty with her dirty shoes."

Daddy: "And now you can see the mayor's castle. And the church with the tower."

Josette: "Ding, dong, ding, dong . . ."

Daddy: "And then you can see the priest at the very top of the tower."

Josette: "Careful, he's going to fall . . ."

Daddy: "No, he's hanging to a rope. He came up into the tower to wave to us with his handkerchief. The mayor and the mayor's wife and the priest's wife are on the tower too."

Josette: "That's not true."

Daddy: "No, that's not true, the priest doesn't have a wife. And now we're going higher and higher and higher . . . Now we're in the clouds, and then above the clouds, and the sky gets bluer and bluer, and now there's only the blue sky, and then down below there's the earth like a ball, and now we're on the moon. We're walking on the moon. We're hungry. We're going to eat a piece of the moon."

Josette: "I'm eating a piece of the moon. It's good, it's very good."

And Josette gives her daddy a piece of the moon. They both eat a piece of the moon.

Daddy: "It's good; it's melon."

Josette: "Let's put some sugar on it."

Daddy: "Just for you, not for me. I have diabetes. Don't eat the whole moon up; we must leave some for other people. Never mind—it'll grow again. Now we take the airplane and go higher again. Higher and higher."

Josette: "Higher and higher."

Daddy: "We've reached the sun. We'll take a walk on the sun. Oh, it's hot. It's always summer on the sun."

Josette: "Yes, it's hot, very hot."

Daddy: "Take your handkerchief and wipe your forehead. Come on, we'll go back down in the airplane. My goodness, where's the airplane? It's melted . . . Never mind, we'll walk down. Let's hurry; we're a long way from home. We have to get home by dinner time or else mama will scold us. We're nice and warm here on the sun, everything is warm, but if we're late dinner will be cold."

Just then mama comes into the room.

"Come on, get out of bed and get dressed."

And mama says to daddy:

"You're going to ruin her mind with your silly stories."

IV

The war in the Middle East has halted for the moment. There is a semirecess. All during the preliminaries of this war, all during the war, all during the aftermath of this war, it was completely impossible for me to write my thoughts down or to write literature. It all seems so vain when there are problems of life and death. I am not so stupid. I always suspected that the cannon was stronger than the pen. But there is no way for fundamental questions not to exist in the human consciousness. Otherwise, there would be nothing, not even the war. The war itself is an answer to a whole set of questions. Those who wage war continue to ask fundamental questions, but they don't know they're asking them. Thus there are those who are good soldiers and wage war resolutely: they have answered one of the "whys" of the endless series of whys. Others continue to wage war out of courage or out of cowardice because they can't stop the wheels from turning, because they don't dare to kick over the traces. They admit that there's no sense to this: they have answered the "why" with an insoluble question. They may be good soldiers. They are courageous cowards.

And finally, there are those rare soldiers who desert: if they don't panic, if they don't give way to a fear greater than that of being punished, dishonored, shot by a firing squad, it's because they are caught up in a justified rebellion against every human, social, age-old way of behaving.

: : :

The three fundamental questions are: "What? . . ." (What is what is?), "Why?" and "How?"

People tell me that adults have given up asking "why?" That is to say, the fundamental "why." They say that this is no longer a question that an adult should ask, that it is a childish question. The "what?" also has to do with the "why?" of course, and enjoys the same lack of consideration, doubtless because it is unanswerable. But one can't help asking oneself these questions that have no answer, and if one does ask them it is precisely because there are no possible answers. If there had been an answer or answers, we would have the answers and wouldn't keep asking ourselves the question.

Serious-minded men, those who are called "adults," say to themselves: "Well, this is the way it is, this is a given fact, we don't know what it is, let us make our peace with what is, let us settle all this, let us make our peace with each other." But in the name of what would they make their peace? And why would they make their peace? What right have they to have criteria? And what's more, they don't settle anything. This is obvious. History escapes them. They want to do one thing, and something else happens. They force themselves to act reasonably. Passions carry them beyond such reasonable behavior. What are passions?

Something that answers to other reasons than reason, reasons that they are not aware of, that are not reasonable, or clear, reasons that they would do better to give in to altogether. To let themselves go. To let themselves go for whose sake? For their own sake, since our passions, our repressed desires are what is most ourselves. What is society? Why is society? The history of the world is made by people who ask themselves fundamental questions but give bad answers, or else refuse to go to the end of the question that does not have an answer, to go as far as possible into the insoluble "why" and instead get stuck in the "how."

The fact that History escapes us, that we do otherwise than we wish to, is obvious. One politician already had some notion of this: Lenin. He said: "History is crafty." This means that he realized that he was not the master of History. And since History is what we make, this means that we are not the masters of what it clearly and consciously seems to us we wanted to do. It will soon be the fiftieth anniversary of the Russian Revolution. This revolution set out to be a liberation, to bring about a better society. It was fifty years of catastrophes, of wars, of crimes, of tyranny, of misfortune; never has a movement that wanted to free humanity of its alienation ever alienated humanity more. In fact, it is not fifty years of revolution that we are going to celebrate, but the birth and the expansion of an enormous imperialist power. In reality, that is what "they" wanted in some obscure way without suspecting that this was so. But all this that I have just said is only a passionate parenthesis. I go back to what I was saying before. I mean, then, that those who stick to the "how" are more or less mental cases. The "how," moreover, becomes a "doing," and "doing" cannot fail to lead to a "why," for "doing" is not circumscribed; it cannot be isolated from a limitless context: it keeps on going, it never stops. People want to create a good society, a better society, but people cannot help but ask why they want to create a better society, and what a better society is, and why one society should be better or worse than some other. And what it is that surrounds me or seems to surround me. If one accepts the "why," that is to say: "Why has this been (done)?" I don't see what difference there can be, when all is said and done, between the "how," the "why," and the "what."

Or rather, I do see. But then, the stupid and brilliant ideologues are only workers who take care of details, proletarians of the mind, alienated men who cannot fail to be conscious of their alienation, just like the worker who screws and unscrews the same bolt all his life until he rebels, that is to say until he asks himself "why?" until he wants to know the "why of the why," the "why of the why of the why." To restrict oneself to the "how" is to enter the system, to accept being an innocent part of the system, that is, to be a Marxist, for example, to be someone who alienates himself and who closes his eyes and refuses the essential problem, the very problem that one cannot fail to ask oneself if one is not to be absolutely alienated, if one is not to be an ametaphysical petit bourgeois, if one is not to die, if one is not to be frozen, in exactly the way that the petit bourgeois of the so-called capitalist societies is dead, or sleeping, or unconscious, or frozen.

In the last analysis, the "why" and the "how" become one. If I say: "How was that done?" I get the answer: "That was done this way." And then once the thing has been done in this way, something has happened, or something has been done, and it has been done in this way, and then, since people have gone about it this way, since it has been done in this way, this is what we have done and how we have done it. But the moment that there is an "after that," one enters into the realm of causality, and the moment that one cannot avoid the "since," that is to say the "because," one comes back to the "why." Neither the "how" nor the "why" have any end. For even if one were to confine oneself to the "how," and we have just seen that we cannot confine ourselves to the "how," but even supposing we were to confine ourselves to the "how," the "how" has no end, the "how" never stops, just as the "why" never stops. This means that the teleological problem cannot be posed, and we come up against this problem just as much by way of the "how" as by way of the "why." What we mean is that if we wish to avoid the "what," if we wish to avoid the "why," we want to do so in order that there will not be any insoluble questions, since it is not worthwhile to ask oneself insoluble questions, according to some. We think that replacing the "what" and the "why" by the "how" does not allow us to avoid the absolute question, since we answer the question "how" with "this way," and there is thus an infinite series of "hows" and "this ways," just as the chain of "whys" and "becauses" is infinite. Neither the "absolute why" nor the "absolute how" can have any other answer than "I don't know."

Certain Japanese Buddhists and certain psycho-analysts have nonetheless foreseen—psychologically, practically—the problem of the "why," the problem of the "why" of our desires, of our libido. The "why" that

Buddhist disciples sought, or were required to produce, or that the person analyzed by the psychiatrist
was required to produce, became one with the "how,"
which the disciple or the patient answered with a "why"
which at the same time was a "this way," and in this
way the mechanism of desire was taken apart and re-
duced to nothing. When a psychoanalysis or a Buddhist initiation succeeds absolutely, which is practically
impossible, desire is totally neutralized; it is "not willing" that ensues.

: : :

The only possible answer is still to answer by a nonan-
swer, knowing full well that there is a question, being quite
aware that there is a question. We are here. We don't know
what that means. We don't know what the fact that this
means nothing means. We are born duped. We don't know
what it means to "be duped." We have only to gaze with
astonishment at cities; we can only look at the ocean. The
only thing to say is "What?"

: : :

There are certain people who are not bothered by vacuum
cleaners, the noise of cars, chairs that are rickety or tip,
which they find uncomfortable to sit on; there are also
people who do not see the houses that are beautiful or ugly,
who accustom themselves to heat or cold, or to being neither
hot nor cold; there are people for whom the outside world
is a matter of indifference; they accustom themselves to it
or fail either to accustom themselves to it or not accustom
themselves to it. As for me, everything grates on my nerves.
I am never comfortable. They say that I have a dreadful
character, but I'm not cut out for that role. Or rather, I
have the profound feeling that my condition of being in the
world is absolutely intolerable.

: : :

I have been given a very bad role. Perhaps I was cut out to be a spectator. Instead of being a spectator, they've made me act in the play. Not even the main part. Not even a real role. I'm a silhouette, a measly bit player. The bit player can't see the whole show; he is not aware of anything but a few strings being pulled, he is familiar with nothing but a few places backstage, the director who lords it over him, his old halberdier's uniform, a square yard of the stage. I'm one of innumerable bit players. Or else one of those numerous bit players that plays the part of prisoners. I have only one line to say.

: : :

I keep thinking of my step-family, My father's second wife, the cousins, the brothers-in-law, the sisters-in-law, the niece of this unspeakable wife, whom he called "Lola."

My father was a lawyer. He didn't appear before the bar. He prepared briefs. He had other lawyers who went to court. He was very clever, it seems. He had left Paris and gone to Bucharest in 1916 to fight in the war, it appears. He didn't fight. He was as strong as a bull, but he was let out of the army. That is not what I have against him. I don't bear him a grudge for having left us and separated from my mother either. One can feel like having another woman. What I hold against him is having done this in the rottenest sort of way. After a certain time, there wasn't a word from him. I was very small. My mother had to work in a factory to feed me. Since it was wartime, there was no way to correspond with people in Bucharest. My mother thought that my father had died at the front like everyone else. Then the war was over. And for years my mother, who had gotten accustomed to supporting herself on the little jobs she had, and also didn't care anymore, didn't try to find out what had become of him. Then suddenly she took steps to find out:

she wrote to the Romanian Minister of War, to the city hall, to the police. And in fact, far from being dead, he had become the chief of police. He had gotten a divorce and married Lola. He had claimed that my mother had gone abroad, and that she had therefore abandoned the family domicile. At the time, it appears, one could take the train and go anywhere one pleased with minor children. In any case, I don't think a passport was needed. In order to win the divorce case, he had committed forgeries: among others, he had forged the signature of one of my mother's sisters, who knew what had happened. The most troublesome part of the whole thing was that it was my father who had gotten the divorce and had also gotten custody of his children, my sister and me, to Lola's despair. By law, my mother had to turn us over to our father, who came to get us. Since my mother had lost the case and since we were legally in my father's custody, my mother received no alimony. Or rather, she did, because a month after our arrival in Bucharest Lola kicked my sister out. She left in tears, with her belongings in a bundle on her back, and went to my mother's. I stayed. This is the only concession Lola made her husband. But at seventeen I also got out and went on my own, finishing my studies, getting a university degree in letters, and feeling very happy that I was free and didn't have any parents on my back. My father, however, was now obliged to pay my mother minimum alimony since he had kicked his daughter out of the house. He didn't pay it. Or else we had to send the sheriff after him, and that cost too much.

My father's second wife was quite a handsome woman, with a fair complexion and nice eyes but very ugly legs and enormous feet. But with long dresses it didn't matter if one had ugly legs. From time to time my father would rebel.

All of us—my father, myself, his wife, his brothers-in-law and sisters-in-law all lived together in the same house. When my father yelled at his wife, she would come downstairs in tears and complain to her brothers. He would come down after her and the brothers would jump him. He was strong and would put up a good fight. But since there were two brothers and they had two or three other husbands of his wife's sisters who were always around on their side, he would come out of the fights they had with black eyes. Lola agreed to come back, but only after having obtained important concessions: never having my sister back in the family under any circumstances; shoving me off into the room the farthest away from the rest of the apartment, making me eat lunch or dinner all by myself, before or after the festive dinners, with the wine flowing freely, that were attended by the whole family, the brothers-in-law, the sisters-in-law, nieces, cousins, and cronies, that is to say second-rate functionaries, members of the police force, and officers of the lower ranks.

My mother tried to bring suit against my father. It was impossible. He had gone back to being a lawyer after having been the chief of police. When my mother brought suit, she found the letter with my aunt's false signature in the archives as part of the record of the trial. My aunt was ready to testify that her signature had been forged. My mother confronted my father with the story of the letter. My father went to the court, bribed an employee, and the famous letter disappeared from the record: there then was no proof of the crime he had committed. Except that there was: the few letters that my father had been able to send from Bucharest to Paris, just after his return, after the complete cessation of mail service due to what was happening at the time. But all the lawyers that my mother contacted lost their nerve one after the other after the visits my father paid them. No, no, they couldn't do that to a colleague, they couldn't put a colleague in prison. The case was never appealed.

When I am told that Socialist justice does not exist and that in a Socialist state it is cynical force and arbitrariness that make the wheels go round, I am quite ready to believe it. I find it hard to believe that bourgeois justice was any better, at least in the countries in Eastern Europe where it was Socialist tyranny that replaced bourgeois injustice and tyranny. All this merely means that ideologies adapt themselves to tyrannical ancestral habits that go to make up the temperaments of certain people, and that ideologies are helpless in the face of hereditarily acquired manners and morals. Once more, ideologies are only excuses.

: : :

As I reread the foregoing, I notice that I nonetheless have a code of ethics and that I pass judgment. But basically, I don't have any such code. My attitude toward others is merely dictated by the desire to cause them as little trouble as possible. This is what takes the place of a code of ethics for me. But this too is an inherited way of life, a hereditary social habit, what one calls a prejudice perhaps. I no longer know where I'm at. It is obvious from what I said just a moment ago that I have a few memories of Nietzsche left and even a few ideas on the relativity of ethics that apparently come from Marx.

: : :

1967: I reread pages of my private journal. Writing private journals is tantamount, it seems, to succumbing to an unpraiseworthy individualistic temptation. In fact, the "I" is a "we." That is to say, the way I am, the way I think is determined by objective conditions. These objective conditions are lived by a whole social group, on the one hand, and yet in a certain sense only by myself, who nonetheless am part of a social group. When I say "I," it is therefore really both the social group that I express or that we express and a criticism of that group; or else, through the self that says "I," it is objective conditions that I criticize, it is objective conditions that I discuss, that I render explicit. When I say "I," it is only a manner of speaking. In reality, I don't even say "we," I say "that thing."

It is curious to see that all organized collectivities have fought what are called "individualists" or "asocial individuals," that is to say those who are amoral, criminals, madmen, anarchists, and anticonformists, or those who are so labeled. Any society tends to make things uniform. The code of ethics and the established way of thinking are "made uniform." There are countless instances of the battle against those who are asocial. Whether a society is Communist, racist, Catholic, or bourgeois, its aim is to combat those who think differently, those who are different, that is to say those who rebel against the law. Today the extreme right has taken power in Greece. Those who have taken power, like all revolutionaries and all reactionaries, want to put everything in order, that is to say, they want to reestablish authority, that is to say, authority becomes tyranny once again. It becomes a "morality" and becomes moralistic.

As a matter of fact, nothing has ever been accomplished, nothing has ever been changed in the world except by those who are asocial. What is asocial is revolutionary, it is the expression of criticism. This contradiction has always existed: History cannot be made except by asocial individuals, without whom there would be no changes made; at the same time, no sort of society is possible, by definition, with those who are asocial. There must always be a balance between sociability and asociability in order for there to be History. Somehow History and societies find this balance. Societies suppress what gives them their reason for being: criticism. But it is never the same criticism. And this criticism, this anarchy necessary for the creation of a new order is always looked down upon, for it is considered "reactionary" by rightest intellectuals in power.

: : :

My father's two brothers-in-law, Costica and Mitica, had incredibly round faces. They both had little toothbrush mustaches. One was a government employee in the Ministry of Agriculture; the other was a captain, a military prosecutor, then a lawyer. They were completely within the norm. After 1945, when there was a new norm, they were completely within the new norm. They adored the State. To me, power is always wrong. To them, power was always right. This was a sort of sincere, naive opportunism. My father disinherited us. He willed everything, all his property, to his wife's niece. All this niece kept in the end was an apartment because of the Socialist expropriation, an expropriation that I approved twice over. The niece still lives in the apartment she inherited. The captain said that he was going to kill my mother with his saber. They all wanted to have a "good social standing" and be rich. They became rich. My father, my mother, Lola, Mitica, and Costica too perhaps, are dead today. If God wants to forgive them, I'm not against it. But I can't forgive them, I can't forget, there is no good, there is no evil, they were neither good nor bad, they were stupid. They did so many unjust things to me that they have spoiled my whole life, despite what might be called successes. I too have come to the end of my success. In any case, with or without grief, with or without success, all lives are spoiled.

The cat that is three colors—white, black, and brown—goes inside the fireplace where a big wood fire is burning. She first walks around the flames, then goes into a hole on one side of the chimney. It's a pipe.

"Isn't that cat afraid of fire, madame? Doesn't she risk being burned alive?"

"Don't you see how she goes around one side? She keeps away from the flames," the rather young, petite, brunette lady who is on the other side of the fireplace answers, in this room which is half urban and half peasant, resembling both the parlor of a farmhouse, the parlor of the mill at La Chapelle-Anthenaise, and a fashionable drawing room. There are both rustic pieces of furniture and upholstered easy chairs. There's a big rug under the legs of the long farm table and the benches. The room is lighted by the fire from the fireplace and also by a much too narrow window that has been very clumsily cut out in the wall at the very back of the room, behind the lady whose house this is. There is the orange glow of the fire, and from the window there comes a vague, gray light: this window looks out onto the yard with its rabbit hutches and thorny bushes at the other end. Because it is rather dark, I hadn't seen the face of another woman, a visitor, who is wearing a hat with flowers on it.

"Of course, madame. But that poor cat risks having a spark set her fur on fire."

"Don't worry. She's used to it. Animals are very sure-footed, and besides they can stand heat and flames better than we can, you know."

"They can catch fire all the same."

The cat sticks out her head and looks at me in a rather malevolent way. She disappears up the hole.

"The cat goes upstairs through the fireplace, obviously. I can see that, but if the people upstairs light their fire your cat is sure to get burned."

The lady shrugs her shoulders.

Is she really conscious of the danger to her cat? She replies:

"I don't know, I really don't know . . ." Or else:

"After all, what can you expect?"

Suddenly the cat reappears, comes all the way out of the hole, skirts the flames and the smoke sure-footedly, leaves the fireplace, slips between our legs, her scorched tail in the air, miaows in the darkness of the room, disappears behind the furniture, in pain, and tries to find a place to hide.

"You see, the fire was too hot for the cat."

"But cats like heat. It makes me think of my young chestnut-colored cat who's just died, the poor thing. When he was just a kitten, and so cute, he used to sleep in the fireplace, curled up in a ball on the burning coals for hours. When I think of him, it makes me feel so bad I can't hold the tears back."

"You were moaning; you're dreaming and weeping," the lady in the hat says to me.

"Because dreams are true."

"It's barely dawn. Try to go back to sleep."

"I shall try to go to sleep too," says the lady with brunette hair. "Every time you come, you pass your anxieties on to me in your sleep."

"Try to be quiet and go back to sleep; I'm so tired."

1959.

1941: According to Spengler, a culture is born, lives, grows old, and dies like a man. The history of a culture is shared by all the individuals who live and die within this culture; it is a unity that includes all the individuals, is common to all the individuals who are part of it. (*Today, in 1967, sociological theories do not deny, but in fact even seem to confirm this point of view: we are all in the system, whether we want to be or not, and our philosophy, our ethics, our behavior depend on this system or this collective structure; it is thus a question of an extraconsciousness inside of which our consciousness is shut up.*)

It is true that every man is a closed book to anyone else. A man who is born begins an adventure, a unique, individual story, that is more or less an entity closed within itself. All individuals, however, belong to the history of their culture which contains them and enfolds them. Thus individuals, each different from the other, are unified within the superior unity of their culture. Likewise, a society or the history of a culture seems to be separate from other societies or cultures; one may thus be led to think that it is a question of different organisms. But just as for individuals, these cultural organisms form a part of a superior unity: universal History, common to all "cultures," unifies civilizations or societies, just as each society is common to the individuals that go to make it up. One cannot deny individual peculiarities. But similarly, one cannot deny the general history of humanity, universality.

There are innumerable notes that go to make up any one symphony. Two states of consciousness, or two different ages, both go to make up the same man. Civilizations become unified in the universal History that identifies us. What must be done on all levels is to rediscover the identity, the essential unity, what links us together, what unites us, to discover the movement common to all peoples and all times in universal History, to go beyond the frontiers, the limits. (*In 1967 we would say it is necessary to find a common language.*)

Spengler's philosophy of culture is, as he himself says, a German philosophy. As a matter of fact, it is merely Prussian. Spengler's philosophy is provincial. The French mentality is a way of thinking that could be called "universalist." Spengler's thought asks you to be merely yourself. It is this negation of the universal that I don't like in Spengler. To be oneself does not prevent one from being universal. It is necessary to emphasize what makes us identical, not what separates us. (*1967: That depends; sometimes the differences are more interesting than the resemblances. This is true, for example, in the case of works of art.*)

: : :

The experiences of the mystics have always been exactly the same, independently of the eras and the societies or the cultures in which the mystics have lived. There is no fundamental difference between the mystic thought of Simon the Areopagite and that of Saint John of the Cross, between Ecclesiastes and Saint Theresa, between a Brahman and a monk on Mount Athos. For all of them ecstasy comes into being in the same way; in all of them there is the same impossible attempt to tell us of the ineffable experience; in all of them there is the same vision of light, the same contemplative wholeness of vision. The Christian mystics speak to you of the rediscovery of oneself in God or the Universe, exactly like the Hindus for whom the *atman* is at the same time oneself and the Universal. This is something, therefore, that goes beyond the whole history of the various cultures; a rediscovery, an essential identity of experience beyond individual frontiers as well as beyond collective groups; the Image of the world of the great mystics is the same above and beyond every century and above and beyond all geographical location. One single intuition.

Will I see France again next year? Will I return or won't I? What is going to happen? I ask myself this in terror, but also with just a little measure of hope. Will we be saved? Will I still be alive next year? Will I be free or in prison? Will I still be here, will I still be right here?

: : :

This year a new state has disappeared: Yugoslavia. The Greeks defeated the Italians, and then the Germans defeated Greece. They are occupying the country. Italy has lost West Africa. The Germans and the Italians have been driven out of Cyrenaica. The Iron Guards have taken power and then lost it. The defeated French are beginning to war again as best they can. They don't like the Germans. The Germano-Russian hostilities have begun, which no one expected. The Germans, after enormous successes, have finally met their first defeat. Finland and Romania have declared war on Russia; for the moment, the Romanians have taken back Bessarabia and Bukovina, which the Russians had occupied. After having been attacked by Japan, America has entered the war. The United States' entry into the war has not brought many results for the moment: the Philippines are in the hands of the Japanese. Dutch–Anglo-American possessions in the Pacific are lost.* The Anglo-American navies have undergone disastrous losses. In Germany, Hitler is taking personal command of the armies on land and declares that the final, culminating point of the war is at hand.

: : :

---

* At this point in history, it was to people's liking that the Americans were "so far from home." What were they doing in the Philippines and Indochina anyway? They were doing good things. And now, in Indochina? Bad things. They saved France twice, in 1918 and 1940, and Europe once, including even Russia. This is much too much; they deserve to be hated!

How to accept oneself? If one can't, one has to go outside oneself. How can this be done? By trying to take a look around perhaps.

: : :

For the moment (July 1967) there is practically no more war in Israel. A few skirmishes here and there. Everyone was joyfully prepared to deplore the massacre of two million six hundred thousand persons. The victims did not allow themselves to become victims. Those who were bent on killing were disarmed. Because of this, of course, those who go by the name of intellectuals began to side with the Arabs, especially when it became more and more evident how willing anti-Semite Russia was to take the side of the Arabs, that is to say of their leaders. Certain Arabs would prefer not to go along with all the other Arabs, and from what people who have come from Tunis have told me it seems that the Tunisians are living in fear of being attacked by the Algerians.

Z. tells me that Sartre, who believes himself to be the guide, whereas he is only the reflection, of a certain dominant leftist petit-bourgeois mentality, just as there was also a dominant rightist petit-bourgeois mentality before the war, condemns the Israelis or at least is ready to condemn them for having attacked first. He says that they are the aggressors. Z. replied that if the Israelis hadn't attacked the Egyptians were all ready to do so. That's not the way the problem should be judged, Sartre answered, for "if's" don't mean anything. No one knows what they would have done. "If's" don't mean a thing.

As a matter of fact, the Egyptians did attack, ideologically and strategically. When the North Koreans attacked South Korea in 1950 and the South Koreans, along with the Americans, merely answered this aggression, the Communists said that the North Koreans had only attacked the South materially, whereas ideologically and strategically it was the South Koreans and the Americans who had attacked. The words "ideologically" and "strategically" do not apply today either to the Egyptians or to the Israelis, but for months the Egyptians prepared ideologically, strategically, and propagandistically for a holy war. Moreover, their armies were directed against and were entrenched on the Israeli frontier. It is very difficult to make heads or tails of the whole affair. In fact, it is sometimes the ideology that is said to be objective, as in the case of North Korea, and sometimes this very objectivity is merely pure subjectivity, an illusion, as in the case of the recent war in the Middle East.

Things have never seemed to me to be as confused as they are today. Ordinarily, however, the State of Israel's right to exist is acknowledged. Not always. In the forefront of those demanding that this state be wiped out are certain Jews themselves. They represent the state of mind and the desires of several parties, of course. But since so many Jews have been massacred, since a whole Jewish culture has been destroyed in Russia, non-Jews no longer decently dare to give voice, and to give voice to themselves, to an anti-Semitism that is concealed under the name of anti-Zionism. But the Jews themselves may very well be asking to be massacred. This is what some of them are asking. In the name of communism, they say, and because, as the cliché would have it, Israel is the valet of imperialism.

Thus there are, on the one hand, Jews who demand, purely and simply, the destruction of Israel in the name of the Socialist idea.

There are, on the other hand, Jews who say hypocritically: "Of course, of course, the state of Israel has the right to exist . . . However, I a Jewish man, or I a Jewish woman, am not Jewish, I don't understand why the state of Israel exists, I am not Jewish, I am French, German, English, Italian, of Jewish stock, of Jewish origin, of the Jewish religon, but in the final analysis I am French or Italian . . ."

There are other Jews, there is a category of Jews that does not like the state of Israel. Thus in the papers I have come across the reproaches that were addressed to the state of Israel: the state of Israel has the right to exist, but the state of Israel does not have the right to exist in its present form because it is a state founded on a religion or on the idea of a nation (but isn't the French State founded on the idea of a nation?), and therefore one of the Jews who has this attitude says, "I am a Jew but I am a lay person."

There is finally, or in additon, a third category of Jews that says: "The state of Israel has no right to existence. We are Jews, in fact, we're religious. The state of Israel is not the New Jerusalem and is not created by the Messiah, because we are still waiting for the Messiah. As Jews, as religious people, we only live in the diaspora, we must live only in the diaspora, the state of Israel is heretical." *

---

* We should all be living in the diaspora. Outside of any and every country! A single country: the one which is different from every other country. (*1967.*)

This is the same as saying that in the end very few people accord the state of Israel the right to exist. This country bothers everybody: it bothers the Russians, it bothers the Americans, it bothers the French who had interests in North Africa, it bothers the Jews who must take a stand, it bothers everybody, because everybody is settled down, or wants to settle down comfortably with his selfishness, it bothers everybody because the existence of something strong, powerful, unarguable always creates insoluble problems.

: : :

Around 1940: I predict that events may perhaps take place in this way: the Russian counteroffensive is going to last until April 1942; it will have only limited effects, however; in the month of May, the German offensive will begin again. The Soviet army will be defeated in the autumn of 1942. On the first of January, 1943, Egypt, Gibraltar, the Suez Canal, North Africa, the Caucasus will be occupied by Germany; a part of India, perhaps also Australia, will be occupied by the Japanese.

In 1943 and 1944 there will be a furious arms race between the Axis and the Anglo-Saxons. Total war, in its culminating phase on a truly world scale, will take place in 1943, 1944, and 1945.

The fate of the world will be decided in 1945 and 1946. There will then be four or five more years of war, perhaps more. I would like to be wrong, but it seems to me that the abscess is not yet ready to burst. Furthermore, not all countries have entered action yet: we have yet to see South America, Portugal, Spain, Ireland, Switzerland, Sweden, Turkey enter. Others. Only half the British dominions have entered the fight.

: : :

The end of January, 1942: As soon as I try to write, the clearest ideas become confused, they flee, they fade away in a fog; what is more, I live in a fog, a thick fog. I advance blindly through the fog, I see only the distorted contours of meanings. I sometimes fish for an idea that slips through my paws.

First of all, our physical life is threatened. An imminent threat; we live in a precarious shelter: it's war for everyone. Moreover, if there were a rebellion of the Iron Guard it would be the end of us (we would be eliminated as men of the left); we would also be wiped out in the case of a Communist revolution (insofar as it was bourgeois); or, finally, we could also be eliminated by measures taken by the legal government against people in our "category."

Not only our physical existence is threatened, but also our moral life, our historical existence, our values, our traditions, our culture. Those who are going to die may possibly console themselves if they are certain that their world is going to survive. It is our intellectual and moral universe that sees the future being closed. This is not at all because History is confused, chaotic, absurd, because it is to be conquered and because its present conquerors have another vision of the world than ours and are trying to impose that vision. We are being driven out of their universe. And even if I were not driven out of it, I could not become part of it, I could not accept it. I would merely choose death, without the hope of a resurrection.

An English traveler left France in April 1789. He returned in October 1789: he said that he no longer recognized France. Everything was completely different: people's faces had different expressions, their way of walking and moving was different, their way of speaking was different, there was another way of thinking, another sort of movement, other rhythms, and even the "outward look of the streets" had changed. There were other signs on the shops, English travelers tell us. But I think there were really other streets, other houses, even though they were materially the same. It was another planet. *There had been a mutation.*

This is what I seem to be feeling right now. The new Romanian men are no longer my fellow men. Nor are the Germans, of course. Nor are the Russians, and perhaps not the French either, perhaps a metamorphosis is about to take place in France too; there is not, there will not be anybody left. They are all of another race, not of another race, but, worse still, of another species than men.

: : :

Yet it is strange. After the collapse of postrevolutionary France, conquered by the Germans, it seems as if the old France, the France of bygone days, the France of before 1789, had been reborn in order to fight. It is as if it had survived in the consciousness of a few individuals.

The very most that I myself can hope for is to be a sad, lonely survivor of my world, a soul in torment, a melancholy phantom. What else can I with my journal hope to be other than an archeological relic?

: : :

There are four hundred intellectual Iron Guard leaders in Germany; through them, thousands of Romanian workers and students are going to be impregnated by the new German thought. They are making preparations, they are meeting, they are exultant, they will doubtless constitute an unusually powerful ferment, the future of the Romanian world of tomorrow.

In Romania there is a philosophical society bearing the name of a Fascist professor and consisting of sixty young philosophers. We know how dangerous, how effective these philosophical societies are. These sixty or seventy ideologues meet together, hold discussions, make preparations: they are "mystics," legionnaires or prelegionnaires, that is to say members of the Iron Guard spiritual family,* germs, ferments; there are seventy of them; they will become a hundred, two hundred, a thousand; they are invading the papers, the magazines. They give courses and lectures at the university; they write books; they talk and talk, their voices cover everything. They are the consequences of History. Their vision of the world is about to win out. We will then be lost.

: : :

To get back to France is my only, desperate aim.

I can still find people of my family, of my species there. (*1967: At this time, we lived on the myth of France.*) If I stay here, I will die of homesickness for my real country. A terrible exile. I am alone, all alone, surrounded by these people who are hard as stone to me, as dangerous as snakes, as implacable as tigers. How can one communicate with a tiger, with a cobra, how can one get a wolf or a rhinoceros to understand you, to spare you; what language can you talk to them in? How can they be made to accept my values, the inner world that I carry around with me? In fact, since I am something like the last man in this monstrous island, I no longer represent anything, I am only an anomaly, a monster.

---

* Codréanu, the leader of the Iron Guard, was as handsome as Guevara, as beloved as Mussolini, or Castro, or Hitler . . . a killer . . . like Guevara . . . and like Guevara a killer who was killed . . . People like only handsome assassins, whether they get killed or not.

Yes, they seem to me to be rhinoceroses. But for them, for them who think they are men, for them I am a scorpion, a spider. How can a hideous spider convince these beings that it shouldn't be squashed?

: : :

If, as certain moderns have it, the author, the creator is illusory and his work is written by others, if one claims that works are only the expression of the manifestation of the collective unconscious, or rather of a present social unconscious, that of a nonhistorical society (for the collective unconscious is one of the extratemporal archetypes), if one claims that others speak, not Beckett, Alain Robbe-Grillet, or Ionesco, how does it happen that, in order to speak of the collective unconscious that purportedly is none of these authors, one speaks of Beckett, Robbe-Grillet, or Ionesco to designate the collective unconscious, and how does it happen that the works are signed, that is to say that they are Beckettian, Robbe-Grilletian, or Ionescian: how does it happen that all these authors are different, that they have their own particular stamp, that their works are personal, and that the "I" is illusory?

Is the "I" as illusory as all that? There are collective structures, there is a fabric made up of aspirations, obsessions, desires, needs, general anxieties; there is also the personal and unique structure that an irreducible person gives to these anxieties, desires, obsessions, etc.

Psychology points out that temperaments are different. Psychology, medicine, literary criticism are merely statements confirming the existence of differentiations. One need only walk down the street and look at other people to know that everyone is different from everyone else.

In today's attempt to depersonalize people, in this predilection for collective life whereby an attempt is made to drown man in the nation, in society, in race, I see the consequences, and the fruits, of both Communist totalitarianism and the totalitarianism of certain forms of Nazism.

A new personalism is doubtless possible. Emmanuel Mounier had already defended and justified the person over and above the totalitarianisms of a quarter of a century ago, against these same totalitarianisms. For the renewal of today's personalism, we would have to face up to the neocollectivisms that are being born anew of their ashes with new and doubtless more powerful ways of going about things.

If the person is illusory, why would the nonperson be any less so? In fact, everything can be considered to be an illusion. Everything can be considered to be nonillusion. The individual structure is what gives a form to collective structures. The person is also a form, this form, that is to say an idea, an essence, this essence. That is not an illusion. Everything is related to everything else. There are therefore collective desires, obsessions, anxieties, which have their own way of being, their own dynamic, their own dialectic. I take these collective desires, these collective obsessions, these collective anxieties and give them a system of relations, a dynamism, a dialectic, a pattern, a structure that is mine alone.

I can also "demystify" collective desires and anxieties, and then the collective dialectic itself disappears, as the personal dialectic can also disappear when I demystify the realities of my person, when I discover to what degree they are collective and other than myself.

: : :

There was a time, long, long ago, when the world seemed to man to be so charged with meanings that he didn't have *time* to ask himself questions, the manifestation was so spectacular. The whole world was like a theater in which the elements, the forests, the oceans and the rivers, the mountains and the plains, the bushes and each plant played a role that man tried to understand, tried to explain to himself, and gave an explanation of. But the explanations were less important: what was essential, what was satisfying, was the evidence of the presence of the gods, it was plenitude, everything was a series of glorious epiphanies. The world was full of meaning. The Apparition was nourished by the spirit of the gods, of what can be called gods; the world was dense. Exactly when did the gods retire from the world, exactly when did the images lose their color? Exactly when was the world emptied of substance, exactly when were the signs no longer signs, exactly when did the tragic break take place, exactly when were we abandoned to ourselves, that is to say, exactly when did the gods no longer want to stage a spectacle, exactly when did they no longer want us as spectators, as participants? We were abandoned to ourselves, to our solitude, to our fear, and the problem was born. What is this world? Who are we?

: : :

Around 1940: I have been present at mutations. I have seen people transformed almost beneath my eyes. It is as if I had come across the very process of metamorphosis, as if I had been present at it. I felt them becoming more and more strangers, I felt them withdrawing, little by little. I felt how another soul, another mind germinated in them. They lost their personality and it was replaced by another. They became other.

I., for example. He was part of our group, we were there together, those of us who were trying to resist the others, those who had us surrounded. It was a question of mental resistance. We had to convince ourselves that they were not right; it was a question of finding counterreasons, and these counterreasons had to be real ones. We were young at the time. How could we hold out intellectually against so many specialists who had become fanatics: sociologists, philosophers of culture, biologists who found "scientific" reasons to justify racism, writers, journalists?

There was, in fact, a Marxist biology, there were philosophers, some of the greatest of them, who gave in to the absolutism of the state or to the collective delirium. What could we do?—Meet as we were doing, and try to think among ourselves and to answer, in particular, all the howling radios, all the speeches, all the images, all the books that assailed us. But there were nonetheless some defections. One day I. came and told us that we were right, of course, and that the others were beyond doubt monstrous or stupid. However, he said, it's strange sometimes: they seem, they seem to be right on one point . . . One point out of ten thousand, but all the same, in order to be completely objective . . .

We asked him what the point was that "they" seemed to be right about. I. answered: "When, for example, they say that the Jews . . ."

At that moment we were immediately aware that I. was caught in the cogs of the machine. It was only the first symptom of an incubation that would go on until he had a bad case of the disease. I. already had a strange light in his eyes, whose meaning I could not mistake. We couldn't yield to even one argument of our enemies. The slightest concession and everything was lost. One was irreversibly caught in the cogs of the infernal machine.

There were fewer and fewer of us and I knew how this happened: I gave them between four and six weeks to definitely succumb, to yield to temptation, to the temptation of power, and find excuses for their fear, for letting their arms fall to their sides and not fighting anymore, for bowing within themselves to all the reasons of others and becoming like the others, with great relief. They became men possessed.

I am astonished to see how this resembles my play *Rhinoceros*. This is the real origin of this play. It was only very recently, when I went back to the pages of my old journal, that I saw that I had called them rhinoceroses, something that I had entirely forgotten, and it is only by a curious happenstance that I seemed to have rediscovered the name of these adversaries or these fanatics who had become imbeciles. This raving fanaticism still exists today in the form of Communists and Red Guards and so forth . . . it is no longer the Nazis. And as it is no longer the Nazis, they are said to be in the right, with arguments, naturally, that served to justify these others before: it is History that is right, they are on the march with History, there is only sociological truth, etc. As if collective madness could not exist. But now it seems to me that people are waking up just a little bit, as witness the struggle of a few consciences against oppression in Russia, in Czechoslovakia. The tyranny of the new

Algerian government, the murders committed in the Sudan as well as in Yemen by Nasser, the murderous anti-Israeli madness, which are all always supported by "arguments," seem to me to be definite proof that there are murderous collective psychoses, some sort of enormous disorders of History, madnesses, sicknesses . . . If madness exists, of course, for it is perhaps our sanity that is a madness . . . In short, why do people not reread Gustave Lebon, the author who writes on these crowd psychologies, who has been so unjustly forgotten?

: : :

It is as if I had seen transformations. I have seen people being metamorphosed. I have noticed, I have followed the process of mutation, I have seen how brothers, friends progressively became strangers. I have been aware of how a new soul germinated in them, how a new personality was substituted for their old one.

I recently met A. We can no longer understand each other, he is someone else, someone who still has the same name. There was a time, not long ago, when my heart glowed when I pronounced his name, when I wrote his name, when I saw him, or when I thought of him; I felt a warm, comforting presence. Now when I write his name, when I pronounce his name, when I see his face in my mind, I have a feeling of horror, almost hatred, a great discomfort. His name seemed to be that of an archangel. Now this same name is barbarous, or seems to me to be: worse, it's the name of a hyena or a dog.

Some time ago, he lived in a little house in the middle of an immense garden. The garden was guarded by an enormous dog, a bulldog, who was almost wild, very ugly, and possessed of a stupid cruelty. He was tied up during the day; he didn't get along with anybody. He was implacable and ferocious. He was the only really stupid dog I have ever known. He never barked; he silently jumped on anyone, ready to tear him to pieces. Once during the day the dog managed to get loose. A. found himself face to face with the dog. The dog jumped on him. A., screaming, struggled with the dog for a few minutes in a frightful encounter. When the two were finally separated, A. was pale, with the face of another, changed, curiously changed. From that time on, A. began to be someone else. Little by little someone else took his place. The animal had possessed him, it had left its seed in him. I recently met the new A. by chance. I was stupefied, frightened. The germination, the growth, the flowering of the seed of the animal had taken place. Even A.'s face is no longer the same: it has gotten larger, it resembles the dog's. He has become the dog's child, or perhaps the animal's female. He is ferocious, implacable, stupid. One can no longer talk to him. He no longer understands my language, his old language. I said a single word to him, straight out: that he ought to be exterminated. In fact, A. barely looks like A. anymore—A. is only a distant memory.

I nourish the impossible hope of a universal catastrophe that would destroy all of us. It had been snowing for some time, there had been no letup for two or three days. Then suddenly it stopped snowing. It's a great disappointment, because I can no longer hope that snow will fall for weeks and weeks and bury us all. Alas, it is only our despair that is disproportionate; I am lost. I am far, far away, I am plunged in endless shadows.

: : :

Today at the barber's when I looked at myself in the mirror I spied my father's good-natured smile on my lips.

: : :

The geography teacher at the lycée S. S., the teacher who is so kind and so nice, asks me with his usual kind smile:

"Is it true that all the Jews in Bessarabia have been killed? That means that they have begun to put their plan to exterminate Jews into effect. It's none too soon."

And he was happy. I don't know what makes me angrier: their stupidity or their bestiality.

On the street, the owner of a creamery says:

"All this is on account of the Jews."

Then spitting off to one side, he adds with the appearance of having thought profoundly:

"It's because of them that our children are dying."

1967: Today people would say: "It's because of the American imperialists." And if anyone should say today that the Americans aren't the ones who want wars, people would be angry, despite Marxist thought, which as anyone can see is essentially a philosophy of conflict and preaches the necessity of one last war, world catastrophe, upheaval.

How could that fail to be true since it is written in the newspapers? It is frightful to know that everything is controlled by a little group in command, that everything that is written in the papers has a conscious purpose that is unconsciously taken up by others, that poison is fed the multitudes.

M. S. says to me:

"Look at all these people in the streets, they don't have brains anymore, what they have in their place is the mud of propaganda; another sort of propaganda will fill their heads with another sort of mud."

It is so simple, however, to see that the Germans are like the thief that cries "Thief!" that if they say that they are being attacked it is so as to be able to attack, that if they accuse others, the Jews for example, or France, it is because they themselves want to conquer the world. Imagine: Czechoslovakia threatening Germany. And imagine: people believe this. In Bucharest the Iron Guards circulate in serried ranks singing: "The Jews are trying to crush our nation," as if seven hundred thousand persons could smother seventeen million . . .

But I must say that what enrages me most is that, even though I see through it, even though I know the mechanism of propaganda, even though I am conscious of what there is behind it, I suffer like a man in the street, like a man in the crowd. In fact, even though I am curious of what is happening, I can do nothing, I can play no role, I am instead played with. I am in mortal danger, threatened with being wiped out, I don't deserve such a fate, I don't deserve it because *I understand*. I am furious at feeling lost in the formless paste of the multitude. It is worse: if I am still hard, I am going to be crushed, *unless I am cleverer*. You are keeping me here by mistake, I am caught here because of an error. I have other things to do. There are other things I should be asked to do, you're making a mistake, I have my destiny! "They" have made an inadmissible, colossal mistake in assigning me a part in the universe, in this society, in this place! It is certain that somewhere my absence must be causing surprise, must be worrying people. They must be looking for me, wondering, and so on.

: : :

X. wants Germany to win. Not for the same reasons as others. His reasons are different. The Romanian Fascists, who say that they are Christian, maintain that Germany must win because Hitler's Germany in any event is Christian . . . despite itself, unconsciously. In any case, they say, it is not against God, and despite everything it is less anti-Christian than Soviet Russia. X. does not believe these slogans. Nor does he believe the cliché that says that Germany is going to institute "a juster order in Europe," etc. X. is a partisan of Germany and its victory because he is convinced that "Germany is a country that is struggling for its life against the Anglo-Jewish plutocracy that is trying to kill it." So X. imagines that this is a personal thought. He does not realize that all he is doing is adopting different slogans.*

In reality, the reasons one gives for an attitude are not the real reasons. Moreover, these reasons change, succeed one another, contradict one another; the real reasons for an attitude, for an act, are obscure and hidden. A person wants to "defend Christianity," and this permits cruelty, the unleashing of sadism, the will to power. The Iron Guards think that they are saints; they are murderers. We ought to force everyone to be examined by a psychoanalyst.

: : :

Yesterday, literature valued weakness. It seemed to find nobility in sadness, powerlessness, our spiritual misery. Poets moved people to pity. Literature was bad and feeble: mere complaints. Naturally; but today we live in a world of tigers. A universe of fire and steel. When peace comes, it will still be an iron peace. A world powerless to act. A hard, cynical world. And perhaps one that is too lucid.

All the sentimental, pathetic, rhetorical literature of the nineteenth century seems ridiculous and stupid to us. The Victor Hugo of *Les misérables,* with his ideal of charity, social justice, and generosity, makes us laugh as much as the

---

* Thus one was for Nazi Germany for contrary "reasons": (1) because Germany was (relatively) Christian; (2) because she was not; (3) because she was justice; (4) because she was power. As a matter of fact the fourth reason was the most honest. (*1967.*)

humanitarian, rhetorical sentimentality of the Michelet of the *Histoire de la révolution,* as much as the poems and prose of Lamartine.

For some time now Romantic prose has seemed ridiculous and tepid to us. In the face of the new world that is suddenly appearing, the literature of those contemporary writers who seemed the coldest and the most lucid to us will seem to be not lucid enough, not cold enough, and will go down the same drain as sentimental and liberal literature. We are lost. We are no longer contemporaries. But I shall not vegetate, I shall not live a mediocre existence.

: : :

We are anxiously awaiting the attack of the German armies on Russia. Can the Russians hold out? We are also anxiously expecting legal measures that will perhaps provide for our annihilation. C. is convinced that in the end "the old humanistic values will win out because they are eternal." I am dumbfounded. A member of our group who denounces the clichés of others, he himself is now speaking in clichés.

: : :

N. is to be named a lecturer in philosophy at the University of Bucharest. He is a very nice, very refined, very distinguished man, too nice, too refined, too distinguished. He is an Iron Guard. He tells the party militants to be "frightfully good." The "good" here has either the conscious or the unconscious role of hiding the "frightfully." He thus tells them that they must kill with "kindness."

: : :

We are going toward the desert, time is transporting us to the iron age. I look at the recent issues of the *Nouvelle revue française:* it is unbelievable, the NRF is favorable to the Germans. Pitiful shadows, rightist intellectuals, the weak trying to appear strong, Drieu la Rochelle, Brasillach, Petitjean, Montherlant, etc., write that France lacked toughness and virility and that Germany will give her this virility that she lacks.

I read Drieu la Rochelle's stupefying poem, written some time ago: "To you Germans . . . I speak to you through my now unsealed mouth . . . You are strong . . . Let us rejoice in the strength of the Germans . . . When plenitude is attained, let it be suddenly consumed in the splendor of paroxysms . . . Your blood must carry along this new invasion of the grandiose . . . Today, mouth to mouth, body pressed to body, Germany breathes a new ardor into us . . . War gives vent to grandeur, like a virginity . . . May a race die in a charnel house of still-living flesh . . . This is the lot that I would choose for France." (*Anthologie de la nouvelle poésie française*, Paris, 1928, Editions Kra.) We see what this means: when the Frenchman is no longer anything but a sexual pervert, a ragged tatter, neither a man nor a woman, a sort of filthy trash, then France will deserve to be spit on. It will then be garbage . . .

: : :

Last night I dreamed that I was in Paris. I woke up with such a burning pain, such nostalgia! In my dream I saw Paris again, on an autumn day; I was happy to find myself in streets that I knew well; it was raining, but at the same time the weather was fine. I came home, but I lived in ugly, damp rooms that had rotted, so to speak, rooms resembling those that can be found in the sinister suburbs of Bucharest. Worse still, we were moving into a dark basement apartment, in a street that resembled General X Street in Bucharest. I felt very ill at ease. I tried to console myself by telling myself that even if our rooms were ugly, even if we lived on a street in Bucharest, this could have no importance, because once one was outside, at the end of our street, two minutes away, there was Paris. We could not console ourselves however. We were overwhelmed: the ugliness of these two dark basement rooms, the shadows, the dampness, the rain we could see falling on the other side of the window-panes, the darkness could not be overcome. Then a curious thing happened: we had invited a lot of people to our house, among them my father and his second wife. What was he doing at our house? Everybody was there in the shadow or the half-shadow, clad in their raincoats, their coats, their overcoats.

I woke up. It seemed to me that our two rooms in the basement symbolized the grave and that everybody had come to our funeral, or to someone's funeral.

An original and authentic Balkan "culture" cannot be really European. The Balkan soul is neither European nor Asiatic. This has nothing to do with Western humanism. Psychological preoccupations, which are so important in France for example, would be more or less disdained by people in the Balkans. As for erotic sentimentality, it exists in Romanian literature only because it was imported from France or Germany in the Romantic period. Passion can exist, but not love. Nameless nostalgia can exist, but only without a face, unindividualized. And instead of humor, indeed instead of irony, there is only crude, pitiless, peasant raillery. The Balkan peoples declare that they are Christian; they are hardly so at all. They can have a sort of faith, psychological faith, a faith that resembles a decision firmly made. Above all, they are not charitable. Faith for them might be considered not to be a faith at all since it is so different from the emotional, psychological, or intellectual faith of Catholics and Protestants. The priests are materialists, positivists, atheists in the Western sense; they are thieves, satraps, crafty old foxes with their black beards, pitiless and telluric: real "Thracians."

The most admired and most popular Moldo-Walachian sovereign was called Vlad, nicknamed "The Impaler," for impalement was the one death penalty he imposed on thieves, his rivals, the Turkish soldiers occupying the country that he had rebelled against, deserters, merchants, those out of favor, and so on.

The Iron Guard phenomenon is not something temporary; it is profoundly Balkan, it is really the expression of the hardness of the unrefined Balkan soul.

But of course things might be different, everything might change tomorrow morning. Mutations, even if they are favorable ones, are not out of the question. Perhaps there will be a less luminous serenity, perhaps there will be grace . . .

: : :

What a stupid idea for us to have left France! We should have stayed there, even if the country was occupied. I kick myself. Aren't we occupied here? We are even doubly so here, a hundred times more. I am making superhuman efforts to get back to France, or in any case to leave here.

Three weeks ago we had passports and visas. We waited two days too long, in order for me to arrange a leave from the ministry. These two days were fatal for us: Yugoslavia was invaded, and transit through that country obviously became impossible. So we went to the German Consulate to ask for a transit visa through Germany, in order to get from Germany to Switzerland and from there to unoccupied France. I made this latter request with the conviction that I would get no for an answer. A few days ago I therefore went to the German Consulate, where I learned that I had been granted a visa; since a state of war did not yet exist in Romania, the military authorities grudgingly granted me permission to leave. But in any case I did have permission. But I didn't believe in the German visa: salvation was five hundred years from us, in the hands of an embassy secretary.

The German visa has run out now, and my passport as well. I decided to begin all over again and try to get the prison door to open. But I couldn't ask for another visa without a new passport. I've resigned myself: I have just learned that since yesterday the Council of Ministers has decided that no one can cross the borders except on an official mission.

Despair, anger, calm, apathy. How can I have been so stupid? Everything has to be done all over again.

: : :

I read the following in André Gide's *Journal,* dated January 29, 1932: "The idea that so much suffering can be in vain is intolerable to me, it kept me awake all night; I'm awake now . . ." As a good Westerner, André Gide couldn't help but think that suffering was the price of happiness, that suffering had to be rewarded. The Balkan peoples don't "pity" those who suffer. In fact, suffering has no value. The Balkan peoples have, rather, a tendency to scorn it; this is the contrary error. Quite simply, it need not be taken into consideration.

: : :

I think of the lawyer in Bucharest who was one of the chiefs of police of the government which collaborated with the enemy in 1918 when Romania was occupied by the armies of William II. Germany was losing the war; French armies coming for Salonika had entered Romania and joined the Romanian army of General Averesco, who was desperately holding on to a little piece of ground, or fighting heroically in Moldavia against the Germans, against the typhus

that was ravaging the army and the civilian population, and against the depredations of Russian pillagers.
After the Germans had been defeated, General Averesco, a national hero, was asked to assume power.
The members of the government who had collaborated
with the enemy were not shot, of course, and were not
put in prison: they simply went and hid on their es-
tates in Moldavia or Walachia (for they were rich,
conservative landowners). The lawyer did not go into
hiding. He became a member of General Averesco's
party and one of his faithful disciples. Around 1930
or 1935 a new movement came into being and grew,
the only party to go in the direction of History, the
Democratic party of peasant nationals, vaguely Socialist, somewhat Masonic, and rather antimilitaristic.
The lawyer abandoned General Averesco, joined the
national peasant party, and became a Mason. Then
came the Fascist Iron Guard, which won over the entire country. There was a collective delirium, and en-
thusiastic mass support of the Guards; Codréanu, like
Mao, like Hitler, like Castro, like Nasser, was the beloved tyrant, the adored killer, the prophet or the Messiah sent by God to do justice, but above all to kill
and flagellate his enemies and his friends. The lawyer,
still going in the same direction as History, became a
partisan of the Iron Guards and said to his son: "I
have committed one great error in my life: I have
sullied my blood; I must redeem the sin of the blood."
Then came the war; the Iron Guards took power, then
the Iron Guards were thrown out, and a general, the
enemy of the Iron Guards, and also an enemy of the
Russians and thereby an ally of Hitler's Germany, became commander-in-chief of the Romanian armies and
President of the Council: the lawyer was convinced of

the rightness of Antonesco's attitude, condemned the Guards as criminal anarchists, and, still going in the direction of History, joined General Antonesco's cohorts. Germany lost the war, as did the Romanians, the Russians occupied the country, and the Communist party came to power. Socialist order was instituted, that is to say disorder, for everything was turned topsy-turvy. There was no more need for lawyers. The Communists drove all but five of them from the bar, and among these five was the lawyer, who landed on his feet once again, still going in the direction of History. And yet the man was not really an opportunist. He simply had what Jean Grenier called "the spirit of orthodoxy"; he believed in power. He was an instinctive Hegelian: the truth for him was the State, could only be the State, the truth could be none other than the truth of the official journal, or else if it was not the State, it was in any case the most massive and most general power that must be the truth, the truth was history, is history: can there be any other truth than that of history or present power? He was docile, he believed this sincerely; that is the reason why all the parties never reproached him for having been a member of other parties. He had no imagination except for the present. And yet, despite his law studies, he was not at all what is called an "intellectual." He reacted, however, like an orthodox rightist or leftist intellectual.

: : :

1940: An almost unbearable tension. Perhaps we are going to get out. An insane hope. I am terrified at the thought that tomorrow may bring disappointment.

: : :

There is such a thing as flea circuses. The fleas can be trained; the first thing to do is to get the fleas not to jump anymore. How can this be done? The fleas are put under glass. The fleas try to jump, bump against the glass, and fall back down again. After a certain time they won't jump anymore. The glass can be taken away. And the stupid fleas now walk slowly around; you can nudge them with your finger, or blow on them, and they will no longer jump.

I am still trying to give a start or to jump, but more and more infrequently, with less and less conviction. When it is peacetime again, when the borders are open again, when I am given back my freedom, perhaps I will no longer dare to jump for fear of bumping against the invisible glass.

No, of course not, I will still have my reflexes.

: : :

A headache after having drunk too much. Life is not a flower. Shit is. The ragout of orangutan of Rangoon. Rangoon makes the taste of orangutan ragout distasteful. I have burning regrets when, sometimes, I realize that I have tied myself down, that I have bound my hands, put leaden chains on my feet. To be free, to walk, to run, not to crawl anymore.

: : :

I met the sister of B. who committed suicide a few months ago. She has just arrived from Germany. All the Germans in the north are completely fascinated by Hitler. It seems that in Bavaria there are people who protest, who are pessimistic, who deplore the great number of German soldiers that have been killed. The North Germans scorn the Bavarians, but the young Bavarians are as fanatic as the old and young people in North Germany. One cannot talk to young Germans of humanity; it is a word they no longer understand. If you pronounce the word, they look at you in surprise, and don't understand at all. A young German who has just gotten a month's leave is bored at home and impatiently looks forward to returning to the front: war is such a great thing! Another who has been wounded and is now blind declares that when he realized that he could no longer see he was in despair for two weeks. Now, he says, he is used to it and regrets only one thing: not being able to fight anymore. All Hitlerites think that the Poles, the Serbs, the Belgians, etc., must be exterminated because they have not understood Hitler and the new Germany. They are certain that in 1942 they are going to win a rapid victory over the Russians, and then, just as rapidly, over the English. The English will soon be taken care of; gas is going to be used to exterminate them without munitions. They do not deserve bullets.

There are no more baptisms in Germany. A resurrection of paganism, or else religious indifference. The North Germans detest the Bavarians because they are still religious. A young girl invited to a party tells her partner as she dances that her brother has just been killed at the front, as if this were just an incidental piece of news. The very young, who are enrolled in the different Hitler organizations, are frighteningly stupid; they have no more feelings; the way their minds have been formed, or rather deformed, has been a perfect success. All Germans have a deep scorn for everything that is not German. The Romanians, whether they are Iron Guards or not, are the most despised. Only the Austrians, the young and those not so young, are anti-Hitler and protest openly. They are not Germans, they say; they are Austrians.

In Munich there are only a dozen Jews left. All the others are in concentration camps. Why have these few Jews been spared for the moment? The reason is not known. They do not have the right to buy food or clothing. A few old friends discreetly get a bowl of soup to them. D.'s sister has seen two of these Jews hugging the walls, not daring to raise their eyes. Doubtless they are allowed to live so that the Germans may rejoice at their humiliation. The world is a hell. It is, of course, only the beginning of hell.

: : :

We are happy when night falls. We know that we will have peace and quiet until the next morning. We also hope for a miracle; the salvation that will perhaps take place at midnight, or at dawn tomorrow . . . Can I escape from here between now and autumn? I dreamed again last night that I was in Paris. And then in the suburbs of Paris. I had lost my way and wandered away from the center of the city. I was trying to get home but I couldn't; at the end of each street an immense wall suddenly sprang up. I turned around the other way, I walked down other streets, but other walls at the end of the streets barred my way every time. I wandered about for a long time.

: : :

General Antonesco has driven the Iron Guards out of the government and put down their "revolution."

A few hundred or a few thousand Jews were massacred during the three or four days of civil war, castrated, hanged head down, stabbed. Among those who were hanged, there were some whose testicles had been stuffed in their mouths.

We have narrowly escaped falling under the provisions of a great many new decrees, but the greatest danger we will have to live through is right now, this year. What could we do, the isolated few of us without arms and no possibility whatever of becoming organized? What could we do except slip between the rails of fate and dodge the blows? If we are still alive at the end of the year and have not yet been driven mad, we might almost consider that we have won a victory. Let us gain time. If the fortunes of war change, the countries allied with Germany, their governments, will draw back little by little, will make concessions, will place a few of their bets, and then more and more of them, on the other side.

: : :

I can't say that I don't also feel a sort of secret joy when I learn that the port installations in Singapore have been blown up, when I learn that the oil wells in Java are burning, that the Soviet dam on the Dnieper has been destroyed, that entire cities and factories in Russia are only ruins, that entire cities are tumbling down in Germany, in Italy, in England, that millions of tons of shipping of the two adversaries have been sunk, that tens of thousands of Poles, Czechs, and Serbs have been massacred, that hundreds of thousands of German soldiers are dying. It sometimes seems to me that this is not enough.

May the last railway bridge come tumbling down, may the last locomotive in the world explode, may the last airplane fall, may the last bayonet be broken, may we walk on the ruins of all the laboratories and all the libraries of Germany, Russia, France, Italy, England, America; stuffed to the gullet with ruins, I will then go, like Rimbaud, to Africa, among the sons of Ham, amid blacks, on torrid beaches; I will also discover in the desert the most beautiful capitals of the greatest empires. (Literature.)

I am dreaming of an idyll.

Only a fool can still hope.

If only I could get rid of this life. Grace and love are dead. I would root all this out of my heart, and my heart along with it. God or suicide. It will never be spring again.

: : :

Intelligence is perhaps only an inferior form of instinct, a step toward instinct. Only instinct reacts without making mistakes. Humanity is perhaps evolving toward an ant civilization, a sound and stable organization without revolution, and without feeling. Intelligence is still an unorganized instinct, an instinct that is still imperfect. Intelligence is perhaps a transitory mode of adaptation. It will perhaps be transformed into an instinct, and psychological reactions and reasoning into precise reflexes. Organization for organization's sake, the education of groups, collectivisms, slogans, clichés, the handy tags that create reflexes, etc., and "iron discipline" tend to transform the slow, hesitant reactions of intelligence into reflexes. Perhaps bees and ants were once intelligent. They have now gone beyond the clumsy stage of a civilization based on intelligence and have built a perfect, definitive "civilization" based on instinct. The technical, collectivistic civilization of "iron discipline" may lead us toward the world of ants.

Fourth Tale for Children Less Than Three Years Old

This morning, Josette's daddy had gotten up early. He had slept well because he had not gone to a restaurant the evening before to eat sauerkraut, nor had he gone to the theater or a puppet show or to the fair to eat onion soup. He hadn't eaten sauerkraut at home either. The doctor had told him not to. Daddy was on a diet. And since he was very hungry the night before, he had gone to bed very early; for as the saying goes, the man who sleeps is the man who sups.

Josette knocked at the door of her parents' room. Mama was gone; she wasn't in the bed. Perhaps she was under the bed or perhaps in the big wardrobe, but the wardrobe was locked. Josette couldn't see her mama. Jacqueline told Jo-

sette that her mama had left early because she too had gone
to bed very early: she hadn't gone to the restaurant, or a
puppet show, or the theater; she hadn't eaten sauerkraut
either.

Jacqueline, the cleaning lady, told Josette that her mama
had just gone out with her pink umbrella, her pink gloves,
pink shoes, and pink hat with flowers, with her pink handbag with the little mirror inside, with her pretty dress with
flowers, with her pretty coat with flowers, with her pretty
stockings with flowers, with a beautiful bonquet of flowers
in her hand, because mama is very stylish, and has beautiful
eyes, like two flowers. She has a mouth like a flower. She
has a very small pink nose, like a flower. She has hair like
flowers, and has flowers in her hair.

Then Josette goes to see her daddy in the study. Daddy is
telephoning. He is smoking and talking into the telephone.
He says: "Hello, hello, is that you? But I told you never to
telephone me again. You annoy me, I haven't a second to
lose."

Josette says to her daddy:

"Are you talking on the telephone?"

Daddy hangs up. He says:

"This isn't a telephone."

Josette answers:

"Yes, that's a telephone. Mama told me so. And Jacqueline told me so."

Daddy answers:

"Your mama and Jacqueline are wrong. Your mama and
Jacqueline don't know what this is called. It's called a
cheese."

"It's called a cheese?" Josette says. "People are going to
think it's a cheese then."

"No," daddy says, "because cheese isn't called cheese,
it's called a music box. And the music box is called a rug.

The rug is called a lamp. The ceiling is called a floor, and the floor is called a ceiling. The wall is called a door."

And daddy teaches Josette the right meaning of words. The chair is a window. The window is a pen. The pillow is bread. The bread is the rug by the bed. Feet are ears. Arms are feet. A head is a derriere. A derriere is a head. Eyes are fingers. Fingers are eyes. Then Josette talks the way her daddy has taught her to speak. She says:

"I look through the chair as I eat my pillow. I open the wall, and walk with my ears. I have ten eyes to walk and two fingers to look. I sit with my head on the floor. I put my derriere on the ceiling. When I've eaten the music box, I put jam on the rug by the bed and have a good dessert. Sit down on the window, daddy, and draw me pictures."

Something is bothering Josette.

"What are pictures called?"

Daddy replies:

"Pictures? What are pictures called? You mustn't say 'pictures,' you must say 'pictures.' "

Jacqueline comes in. Josette runs to her and says to her:

"Jacqueline, you know what? Pictures aren't pictures, they're pictures."

Jacqueline says:

"Ah, some more of your daddy's silly stories. Of course, darling, pictures aren't called pictures; they're called pictures."

Then daddy says to Jacqueline:

"That's what Josette told you."

"No," Jacqueline says, "she said the opposite."

"No," daddy tells Jacqueline, "you're the one who said the opposite."

"No, it's you."

"No, it's you."

"You're both saying the same thing," Josette says.

And then mama comes in, like a flower, with a bouquet of flowers, in her flowered dress, her flowered handbag, her flowered hat, her eyes like flowers, her mouth like a flower.

"Where have you been so early in the morning?" daddy asks.

"Picking flowers," mama says.

And Josette says:

"Mama, you opened the wall."

V

When Michel Foucault announces or takes note of the end of man, it is really the end of the individual that he is talking about. Man continues to be the measure of all things, whether one conceives of him as an individual or as a totality. Furthermore, whether the person speaking says "I," "one," or "we," it is really "us" that he is talking about. But when he says "we," he also means "I," in somewhat the manner of Louis XIV.

For a long time we have known—I have known, people have known—that we belonged to structures that are larger wholes. If "I" is illusory, it is, of course, because its being is the being of the collective language. I have long felt lost in language. However, it is also certain that there is language in general, on the one hand, and the spoken speech of the individual, on the other. I am not in language in general, I am in the spoken word. My spoken speech belongs to me, my spoken speech is myself.

Language is also somewhat me, because, consciously or not, I assume it.

139

I agree with the idea that structures are, that they change, fall apart, and are reconstituted: structures, or models, or ideas, or archetypes are present, and are invariable in their essence.

Mircea Eliade has remarked that social structures fall apart, become more liberal, and then reconstitute themselves, and this is what he is trying to say, it seems to me, in his *Essai sur le mythe de l'éternel retour* (*Essay on the Myth of the Eternal Return*). This was also noted by Dumézil in his book on *Jupiter, Mars, et Quirinus.*

Thus Michel Foucault's statements are not completely unfamiliar. Revolutions themselves are only the proof of the restructuring of a society that is reestablishing a model, a structure that has partly given way. A hierarchy, a construct, a coherent whole is tyrannically established through revolution, which reinstitutes the essential order: politicians, priests (leaders, ideologues), warriors (in the armed forces, in the police).

If the unconscious plays a large part in the facts having to do with the individual, and in his thoughts, the unconscious also plays a role in the collective action of what people call a revolution; revolution should not be called revolution, but rather reaction, return, restitution.

It is absolutely necessary to be aware of unconscious impulses. Myths having to do with "revolution" must be destroyed.

Every statement is proof of its contrary. Every statement is contradictory. Lupasco has brilliantly told us as much. Thus if one reads *Words and Things* one perceives that the author of this book, or rather, that the particular characteristic of this book is that it was written in an extremely personal way; it is rare to find such clear evidence of the personality of an individual, such an individual style in a text. More than anywhere else, collective language here has served to express a person. Furthermore, collective language is of only statistical or sociological interest; it is the impersonal language of the "one" that Heidegger has talked to us about.

Such a flowering of individual manifestations has never before occurred in political or cultural History —or if it has it has done so very rarely. Those who speak of the end of man have never been as vibrantly alive, and those who say that the individual no longer exists have never manifested his existence as brilliantly.

It is as if those who state that we belong to the whole, to the collective consciousness, freed themselves from it and achieved mastery of it by becoming aware of it. If we become conscious of the unconscious, the unconscious is done away with. If we become conscious of the fact that he who speaks is not *in* his language, we appropriate language, we make language become really "me."

All works are signed. Not only have there never been so many outstanding individuals in the realm of culture and politics as in our time, but also there has never been so much of a desire on the part of so many individuals to show themselves for what they are, to realize themselves.

Nor have there ever been so many dictators and tyrants who have merely imposed their "I" on all the others and made others the instruments of their "I."

One has the impression that it is not the "we" that submerges the "I's" but that it is the "I's" or certain "I's" that drown and destroy the others, the "we."

Obviously, the "I," or, rather, the individual, is the result of drives that come from everywhere; the individual is the product of a society, the individual is conditioned by the collectivity. But each one is a particular case of a larger whole, if not of a universality. And what is important in a work or in an individual is not his resemblance to others but rather his difference, his originality, his uniqueness, his irreducibility. What is important is everything that I do differently from the others. It is a cliché to say that "nobody resembles anybody else." It is also a truth.

It is also true to say that "everybody resembles everybody else." This is man's contradictory truth. If I am determined by the whole, these wholes are also the reason behind many very complex conditionings. It is a widely accepted principle that wholes differ and are irreducible: there are only analogies between one culture and another, but there is no common language; there are watertight compartments, as O. Spengler noted quite a while ago. This is what Monsieur Barthes or any other Marxist would say today, with the difference that Spengler located his watertight compartments in space, or else *also* in space, with Greece here and Egypt there and India still farther off, whereas the Marxists locate them within time and causality, as the result of various breaks stemming from social upheavals that in turn are provoked by the class struggle, which seems to me, all in all, to be a more linear and more simplistic vision of universal

History, whereas the historical vision of Spengler seems to be richer, more various, and less simple.

Of course the individual is motivated, is determined, by the collective, by the universal. And even his "unique" reactions can be explained in terms of conditioning by the whole. The "I" in this view is only the crossroads of many different drives that come to him from elsewhere. But wholes too are conditioned, that is to say, behind the collective there is something supercollective, something extrasocial that conditions it, determines it. In this case, the whole too is illusory since it can be taken apart, that is to say analyzed, by the understanding.

Thus the "I" is no more and no less illusory than the whole. One can at least say in favor of the individual consciousness that it is a much more tenacious, more constraining illusion than the illusion of the whole. We know that the conscious is determined and conditioned by the unconscious. But the unconscious is itself conditioned by a superunconscious, by nothing less than a universal, a universal determination by the universal.

It is in this universal, in this extra consciousness, that I discover myself to be me with regard to what I have that is essential: this is my ultimate essence.

Don't we here come across what Indian thought has called the *atman*? This *atman* might be something like an extra consciousness or a consciousness beyond the consciousness in which I participate, which is my real "I." Thus there is an identification between me and a universal beyond the social collectivity that is as temporary as the individual "I." The essential "I" is beyond culture, beyond History.

It participates in this intelligence or active unconsciousness, this lucid unconsciousness or divinity that leads, directs, and conditions everything, the whole of wholes.

: : :

Roman Jakobson says that the universal structures of all languages can be found in every particular language. He also says that we must conclude from this that languages are at the same time autonomous and interdependent in a more or less natural way, that a language can be studied historically, and that there can be such a thing as the study of a language through the description of a static structure. Obviously, he also says, the wholes shift, but they do not shift from one day to the next; they shift only very slowly.

So there is both synchronism and diachronism. We must realize, he goes on, that human language is both biological and cultural, whereas the language of animals is purely biological. Thus a child speaks Norwegian if he lives in a Norwegian milieu, Portuguese if he lives in a Portuguese milieu, whereas the dog does not speak Norwegian or Portuguese but, like all dogs, speaks only dog language.

I am astonished at the enormous scientific importance attributed today to these truths which in the last analysis are quite simple. Jakobson tells us—and this is a stupefying thing, the only stupefying thing—that the philosophy of language has existed only for a relatively short time, that linguists have been wondering what linguistics is for only about half a century. What can they have been doing up until now? Imagine doctors finally getting around to wondering what medicine is. But linguists had never wondered what language was. It is as if they had only recently become aware of the fact that men speak. They didn't even know that language was thought. We really ought to ask only artists and poets for new things and profound truths.

: : :

The Moderns

A refusal of metaphysics. Metaphysics can lead to God. But God alienates us, they say (whereas he is the living sap, the power, the source of the universal energy that we share and participate in). They want nothing to do with anything behind appearances. They would have us see only "society"—let us say, social organization—behind phenomena. Thus for the individual—let us say the "individual soul"—there is no recourse above and beyond social alienation: the social is what transcends the individual. But being as it is the last recourse, the social is what alienates us. That is to say, "the social" is equivalent to "the social organization of a historic time."

But never have there been such great thoughts on the part of individuals than in our era that sings hymns to totalitarianism; never has there been such a great will to power (*libido dominandi*) on the part of individuals in the sphere of politics, culture, and even sports. Interesting contradictions.

Furthermore, if the individual is *determined* by society, society too is determined. What is the great determinant?

: : :

Man, Claude Lévi-Strauss says, finds himself between two societies, the society outside of himself and the society of his millions of molecules, which is just as dynamic a society, one just as full of conflict.

But the "I" is what is conscious of this; it is what integrates this whirlwind. Each "I" is unique. "Individual man" exists, even though he is only this consciousness, only this point of view.

Amid biological and physiological determinations, on the one hand, and cultural determinations on the other, I am here. What is more, other drives determine biology, physiology, psychology, culture. In the last analysis, all the cosmic or metaphysical drives are only my own drive and my own will.

: : :

In all the time that people have been talking about collective destinies, of the collective unconscious, there have never been so many personal wills to power, to knowledge. It is as if each individual, through his thought or through politics, was determined to manifest his personality in order to get the upper hand over this unconscious and these collective entities. There have never been as many lucid personalities trying to become aware of the unconscious, there have never been as many dictators or tyrants, as many unique and irreducible persons.

: : :

This chameleon adapts himself to circumstances. He turns every color, one after the other. But he remains a chameleon. The chameleon merely changes appearance. This leaf is tossed hither and yon by the winds, yet it is the same leaf. What is the "I"? It is the consciousness of being me.

: : :

I am so thoroughly aware, so sure of being myself, among others, but above all myself, that no one can take away this stubborn illusion of mine. The "I" is stubborn. The illusion is reality. The only true thing is illusion. No one is like anyone else. Everyone is like everyone else. This is true too. The unique and the universal coexist. This "everything" and this "unique thing" penetrate each other so little. I have always been. I take others into consideration, of course; I am kind enough not to deny others their existence. In their own way, they have made me; everything has made me. And I in turn make everything. Tell anyone you meet that he does not exist: he will rebel. Am I forever? In any case, I will have been. There is no time; what has been is therefore forever. There are only individual selves; they are, of course, together. If I am, once and for all, this means not only that I am what is universal but that in the universal I am this person, not someone else.

: : :

When we are told (Lévi-Strauss) that the "I" is a complex, a whole composed of thousands of cells and (though he does not say so) dozens of contrary drives perhaps, which are dynamically opposed, and that the individual is only the synthesis or the consciousness and the conscious-unconscious unity of this whole, of this psychobiological society, he means by this that personality is illusory and temporary.

But since the society outside of us, composed of hundreds of thousands of individuals, etc., is as temporary (everything changes, evolves, without changing) and illusory, this is tantamount to saying that the individual "I" is no more and no less justifiable, real, illusory, and valuable than the collectivity.

September 30, 1966: André Breton was one of those creatures whom one cannot imagine not being immortal. It had been some time since I had seen him. I had not quarreled with him. Usually people stopped having anything to do with him because they were angry with him, or, rather, because he was angry with them.

In my case it was different: his presence intimidated me. He was always extremely kind to me however. In any event, I knew that he was there. He had been there as long as I could remember, ever since I had first heard the words "poetry" and "literature." Now it is as the walls and the vaults of a great swatch of my sky had collapsed, along with all their stars.

Why did we love him so? Not only because he had given a sort of fourth dimension to poetry, that is to say to the mind or to one of the manifestations of the mind, not only because he had reinvented literature, as Freud and Jung had reinvented psychology, as Einstein had reinvented physics, as Kafka had reinvented religion, but also because he was the personification of dignity and nobility.

He did not live amid contradictions, but amid paradox. This theoretician of the irrational enlarged, deepened, increased reason; irrationality thus appeared to be something like the hidden face of reason that consciousness could explore and integrate.

In fact, he was lucidity itself. The standard bearer of Revolution, he realized very early what tyranny, what censorship, what constraint, what "realistic" mediocrity were hidden beneath the name of contemporary revolutions. An enemy of fatherlands and nationalisms, he did not play the nationalist game as the antinationalists did (and still do), since they admit all the nationalisms of others. He did not deny France, as the "left" and the "right" did, being just so many thinkers seduced by Nazi Germany at the moment that it pounced on his country, or by Russia at the moment it allowed Nazi Germany to throw itself on the West.

An enemy of poetry, he allowed poetry to exist, as we have said above, and allowed the poetry of his country to permit the existence of a new, universal, young poetry. But we know that he wanted poetry to be life, he wanted us to live in a poetic state of grace, of spiritual tension, of lucid ecstasy that would multiply the powers of the mind ten times over, for though he was an enemy of religion, in which he saw nothing but a sort of degraded philosophy or a closed ideology, André Breton was a mystic.

What can techniques, the sciences, teach us, what can they do except name or utilize things, materials whose composition we learn but whose essence remains impenetrable? Breton taught us to destroy the walls of the real that separate us from reality, to participate in being so as to live as if it were the first day of creation, a day that would every day be the first day of new creations.

To be, to exist without being existentialists, for to be an existentialist is to be the prisoner of logomachies, shut up in words while being escapes us. To live like a revolutionary, that is to say to become aware that revolutions are only enslavement; to be free, yes, to be free above and beyond realisms dogmatically separated from the real. This is what the Surrealist requirement that we participate in being means. From time to time consciousness wakens. From time to time this fundamental requirement of the mind causes its voice to be heard. André Breton will have helped, and will continue to help men to hear it.

Around 1940: My friend Marcel was a sort of would-be superman who didn't quite make it. Being a man wasn't enough for him. A success or a "social" triumph were not enough to satisfy him; if he had wanted to be content with human limitations, he would have been closer to sanctity, he would perhaps have known joy.

It is true that a person who has not completely lost the memory of paradise, even though it is a faint one, will suffer endlessly. He will feel the call of the essential world, will hear the voice that comes from so far away that one cannot find out where it comes from, a voice that cannot guide him. Certain people, carried along by a nameless nostalgia, imagine that it is a land on this earth that they must discover. The conquistadors who wandered over the oceans, on the other side of which there were the Indies and America, left, when all is said and done, in search of paradise. They didn't know that they weren't looking for the Indies, they didn't know that it was the world of the absolute that they wanted. What revolutionaries think they are bringing about is the ideal society, leaving economics and History behind. They do not dare let themselves be aware that it is really paradise that they are looking for.

: : :

Once, long ago, I was sometimes overcome by a sort of grace, a euphoria. It was as if, first of all, every notion, every reality was emptied of its content. After this emptiness, after this dizzy spell, it was as if I found myself suddenly at the center of pure, ineffable existence; it was as if things had freed themselves of all arbitrary labels, of a framework that didn't suit them, that limited them; social and logical constraint or the need to define them, to organize them, disappeared. It did not seem to me that I was the victim of a nominalist crisis; on the contrary, I think that I became one with the one essential reality, when, along with an immense, serene joy, I was overcome by what I might call the stupefaction of being, the certainty of being, the certainty that the social order, politics, language, organized thought, systems and systematizations, limitations and delimitations were pure nothingness and that the only true thing was this sensation or this feeling or this assurance that I existed and that this "I exist" was wholly sufficient unto itself, and freed of everything that was outside of it. I knew that nothing could prevent me from being, that nothingness or night or doubt no longer had any power over me.

I say that with words that can only disfigure, that cannot describe the light of this profound, total, organic intuition which, surging up as it did from my deepest self, might well have inundated everything, covered everything, both my other self and others.

Often this began in an unexpected way, when I would pronounce the most ordinary word: paper, for example. It was as if the word disappeared, a word that had replaced a reality that it had imprisoned and hidden. Or when I would say Aristotle: Ar-is-tot-le. The word "notebook" didn't mean anything, it was only a skin, and the syllables Ar-is-tot-le became sounds devoid of meaning, like a box that had been opened and emptied. This was only the first step. Once I became totally conscious that meanings, that words are arbitrary, mere labels, the nameless man above and beyond categories unveiled himself in his reality and paper had nothing at all to do with school, literature, the stationery store where I had bought it: everything became an ineffable reality in itself, independent of any rational system.

All that—how can I put it?—all these states of consciousness were born in a nimbus of light: around noon, for example, in the month of June or April, on a clear morning. Or once, on a May morning, just before noon, a day that

seemed full of sap, in a leafy park where the light streamed
down, white, blue, green: that day it all began with a senseless, inexplicable joy that I have never again felt so con-
cretely, so carnally, so obviously a *joie de vivre* sustained
by an indescribable astonishment at being alive. As a matter
of fact the consciousness of being and the astonishment at
being were one and the same thing. I suddenly woke up—
from what sleep?—I woke to a light which dislocated the old
meanings of things, of the time when my consciousness had
gone to sleep. The intense astonishment that took possession
of me was only the realization that I was. There was no more
fear, no more anxiety, only calm, certainty, joy. Either
abandoning or waking from a sleep peopled by the phantoms of everyday existence, I suddenly entered the heart of
a reality so blindingly obvious, so total, so enlightening, so
luminous, that I wondered how I had never before realized
how easy this reality was to find and how easily I found
myself in it. How can one not be anxious, how can one not
feel lost and distressed, I said to myself, if one doesn't know
this, if one is not at the very center of this astonishment?

So though the first step of this state of consciousness began with an emptying of the content of notions, the second,
the essential step was a unified plenitude beyond definitions
and limits.

: : :

When I have had insomnia at night, I have never experienced a similar state of consciousness. When I have waked
up at night, I have never been overwhelmed by an astonishment at being. Lucidity at night is made up of distinctions,
of precise divisions, of exact limitations of realities; it is a
lucidity, a clarity that is applied to objects, to things, and
outlines their contours. At such times, definitions and chains
of reasoning are clear and rigorous; it is as if intelligence

were a lighthouse that sees in the dark and lights it up, without leaving the night, which it tears apart bit by bit. Or it's as if intelligence served to shed light on the "what's the use of it all?" with cruel precision, accompanied with an implacable, clear, empty anguish. What is apparent to me in the lucidity of nighttime is things falling apart, death. And all of this would seem to be an infallible logic, a unique certainty. Even if my lucid gaze in the dark turns to objects of little importance, their insignificance takes on such force, such relief, that these objects in the end become prey important enough to hear the call of nothingness. Usually it is the pessimistic light of night that accompanies me all day long.

It seems certain to me that the feeling of plenitude comes into being in and by the presence of light. It is also certain that it is darkness, night, shadows, the absence of light that give rise to negative lucidity.

All light is not real light and not every dawn is grace. Every day, except during a few moments that are so infrequent that I can count them, goes by, like every night, between daylight and darkness, in a gray light, the same old dirty gray, for many days each like the other. I live in a grayness that for such a long time, for as long a time as I can remember, has been interrupted only rarely by the negative lucidities of the night or by a dream that reveals my desperate thirst for the light, for the plenitude that reveals our separation.

: : :

The luminous images of the mystics reveal a full and luminous extra consciousness on which shadows or nothingness have no hold. This is why the feeling, the consciousness of "being" is expressed in images of light, and it is also why light, presence, plenitude are synonyms of "spirituality."

Initiation means illumination, the dispersion of shadows, nothingness held off.

Thus the plenitude that I felt was perhaps a little like mystic plenitude. It began with the feeling that space was emptying itself of its material heaviness, which explains the euphoric sense of relief that I felt. Notions were freed of their content. Objects became transparent, permeable; they were no longer obstacles and it seemed as if one could pass through them. It was as if my mind could move freely, as if there were no resistance to its movement.

Thus my mind could find its center again, reunited, reassembled out of the matrixes and limits within which it had been dispersed. And it was from this moment on that the feeling of plenitude took hold.

: : :

I remember myself walking one summer day around noon in a little village in the provinces in the sunshine, beneath a deep, dense sky. It was a little street, bordered with little white houses whose immaculate walls shone so brightly that they seemed to want to disappear, to melt together in the intensity of a burning, pervasive, total light that was trying to escape from the forms that contained it: in the presence of such light the world seemed about to efface itself, to fade from sight.

Suddenly I felt as if I had received a blow right in the heart, in the center of my being. A stupefaction surged into being, exploded, burst its boundaries, dissolving the limits of things, breaking down definitions, abolishing the meaning of things, of thoughts, as the light seemed to make the walls and the houses I was walking by disappear. "Nothing is true," I said, "outside of this"—a *this* that I was, of course, unable to define, since the *this* itself was what escaped definition, because it itself was the beyond, that which went beyond definitions. Perhaps I could translate this feeling and this *this* by "a certainty of being."

A joy, something more than a joy lifted me up, carried me away. The steps I took seemed to be someone else's, and the sound that they made became as incomprehensible, as inexplicable, as strange as the words that ran through my head, words with no links between them, with no meaning, borne by something like waves, like the scattered wreckage of a ship that has foundered. I watched myself walk, I saw myself walk from outside myself. I said to myself when I saw myself: "So I who am walking on this sidewalk am really the one that I see walking, and what a strange thing, what universe do these houses and these walls and these fences belong to, how all of this is at once the same thing and a different thing; if I wish I can touch this tree, is it really palpable? For what is astonishing is being able to want to or not to want to. I can give myself orders, and I can obey myself; here—the hands, mine, that can do or not do, or loose their grip on each other." Raising my hand to my forehead, I felt how it slowly passed through the air that resisted it. The air had become denser, more compact. The sky, which was made, it seemed to me, of an intermediate substance between air and water, had descended on the city and enveloped me, enveloped all the objects, the walls, and was almost palpable, almost velvet, blue; the deeper and denser the blue of the sky became, the more it could be perceived through the sense of touch, while the whiter the houses became, the less material they became. When I touched my forehead with my finger, I became aware, as if for the first time, of the existence of this forehead. My euphoria became enormous, inhuman. I breathed the air and it was as if I were swallowing pieces of blue sky that replaced my lungs, my heart, my liver, my bones with this celestial substance, somewhere between water and air, and this made me so light, lighter and lighter, that I could no longer feel the effort of walking. It was as if I were not walking now, but leaping, dancing. I could have flown, this depended on just a few things; with a simple concentration of will, of energy, I could have risen from the earth as in a dream or as *once upon a time*.

However, even the pleasure of flight would have been less great than the pleasure I felt at this moment at simply touching my forehead and my chin. And above all neither flight nor anything else could give me greater euphoria than that of becoming aware that *I was,* once and for all, and that this was an irreversible thing, an eternal miracle: the universe merely appears to be, perhaps, perhaps it is only an appearance, but *I am,* I am sure of being. That was completely obvious to me. Everything was merely evidence of this. How blind I had been! What had happened to me, what deep sleep had I been made one with, had I been plunged into? In what nighttime mud, in what damp and putrid substances?

I was saved now. It was impossible for me to become the prey of the mud of shadows again, because I knew now, in a luminous sort of way, I knew and could no longer forget that I am, I myself am, everything is. The miracle of being, the miracle of being, the miracle of being.

I bathed in a warmth, in a gentle tepidness. I heard the barking of a dog, but it was faint and far away, as if it were coming through cotton wool. And in this provincial street that had suddenly been metamorphosed and become beautiful, there was no one in sight, so that nothing in the everyday world could come and shatter the miracle.

: : :

This lasted a very long time. It lasted a few seconds. A cloud hid the sun. The intensity of the light diminished only slightly but that was enough for everything to collapse in

coldness and darkness: for this sordid morning, this morning along with all the other mornings that followed the sur-
real morning seemed very gloomy. The miraculous evidence
vanished. The sky became just any sky. The light or the sun
that had seemed to envelop me drew away from me, took
its astronomical distance once again. Things, the walls,
took on their usual form again; the street became an ugly,
vulgar, provincial street again; the dogs barked noisily. My
lungs took their place in my chest again; I breathed, and
became aware of how painful it was to breathe. All that was
left was this world of ice, or of shadows, or of empty clarity, of gray light, of ashes. It seemed to me that there was
still a corner of light within myself, which I tried to keep,
to enlarge. Alas, everything around me grew dark and everything that had been a sphere or a circle became angles
once again. The everyday world took it usual place again,
and I went back to my usual place in the everyday world.

We are like Cinderella who lived her life expecting a
transfiguration of the world, who lived her life expecting a
few hours of glorious, sumptuous festivities; the rest of the
time we are there in rags, in the dirty shanties of reality. It
is as if we lived in a profound lethargy. We wake up for a
few moments from time to time, then we sink into empty
sleep again.

: : :

Nonetheless, nonetheless the interior mechanism that
can set off this state of supernormal wakefulness that could
set the world ablaze, that could transfigure it, illuminate it,
is able to function in the simplest, most natural way. All one
need do is press a button. Only it is not easy to find this
button; we fumble about for it in the shadows on one of the
walls of an enormous strange house.

: : :

In the history of humanity there are no civilizations or cultures which fail to manifest, in one or a thousand ways, this need for an absolute that is called heaven, freedom, a miracle, a lost paradise to be regained, peace, the going beyond History; there is no era which fails to express the need for man to be transfigured ("the new man," "the superior man," "the superman") or which fails to express the desire for revolution, for the Ideal City, that is to say the desire to purify the world, to change it, to save it, to reintegrate it metaphysically. Humanity has never been satisfied with "reality such as it is." In pagan Greece, where the most perfect harmony seemed to exist between morality and joy, between nature and society, the Platonists, even though they lived beneath the most luminous sky in the world, thought that this world and this sky were only a dark cavern and suffered because they were not able to contemplate the only essential light, that of the eternal ideas. The Stoics themselves passively accepted living an absurd, gray, everyday life because their metaphysics promised that wise men after death would contemplate the movements of the stars, that is to say absolute, nonterrestrial beauty. There is no religion in which everyday life is not considered a prison; there is no philosophy or ideology that does not think that we live in alienation: in one way or another, and even in the ideologies that deny the myths they feed on despite themselves, humanity has always had a nostalgia for the freedom that is only beauty, that is only real life, plenitude, light.

: : :

1940: It seems that a universal storm is driving away the dark clouds of forgetfulness. It is as if humanity were waking up and remembering that it cannot live without the absolute and without perfection. If one translates this into a social and political language, one might say that people are acquiring a "revolutionary consciousness." Those who are moved by this passionate consciousness are, of course, the poor, doubtless because the absence of daily bread arouses in them the obscure and violent memory of the lack of that other, essential, nondaily bread.

In fact revolutions in the beginning are directed against established regimes; the target of revolt is the social organization, all social organization that is only constraint, compromise, routine, impurity, usury. Revolutions deteriorate, and become regimes in their turn. The hierarchy of classes is reinstituted.

New institutionalized morals appear, which wear the beards and the celluloid collars of the morals of yesterday; changes change nothing. What is called life and order— which is not life—hinders life.

Communism itself cannot be understood apart from the myth of paradise. The hidden meaning of revolution is liberation, the desire for a virgin world, the rediscovery of purity through the liberation of man's energies. The Communist revolution is the most painful attempt to liberate and transfigure the world; it is painful and tragic because it is a failure. The Communists are not aware that they have been wishing for a miracle; they believe in the transfiguration of the world by technique, and the biological theories that correspond to political communism are not mutation-oriented without a secret reason. Faith in mutations is the sign that there is an emotional awareness of miracle.

Regimes have always tightened up again. More implacable tyrannies have replaced slack, more liberal tyrannies; a new conformism replaces the old one and humanity falls back into its sadness, into impotence, into sterility; it is "organized" again, and set apart from the solar world, from freedom and joy. I am not the only one to fall back. Humanity falls back. We forget the secret of the gesture that frees, we forget how to go about waking up again; there we are in prison once again, with the chains of the sadness of being men.

Perhaps, perhaps the Great Explosion will be forthcoming. Joy and true freedom will have no end and the youth of the world will be eternal. No stain, no rust spot, no aging process will ever again sully the universe.

: : :

In reality, the upheavals that take place on a political, social, exterior plane are only the sign of our impotence. This is only an attempt at redemption doomed to failure. What we desire, in short, what we wish for on the deepest level, is a transmutation, what we want is to rise to a higher plane of existence. If I had a penetrating eye I would perhaps understand that what I am looking for can be found close to me. I certainly know that, but in an ineffective, exterior way, like something that is said by another person. I don't know it sufficiently, I don't see it myself.

: : :

When I was an adolescent, I was sometimes overwhelmed by an intense, luminous joy: it was an inexplicable, irrational happiness that mounted from the earth, from my feet, and went up to my knees, to my belly, to my heart, to lay hold of all of me. It was as if a light had suddenly gone on in a dark room. Where did this welcome fire that illuminated and purified even the most secret corners of my soul come from? I felt I was in harmony with everything. Everything became beautiful, at once new and familiar. My heart beat faster and I had the impression that I was rising and getting bigger. If I tried to explain the reasons for this extravagant joy to myself, or if I said to myself with false lucidity that I had no reason to rejoice (as if euphoria could justify itself), this state of happiness vanished like a luminous fog and the world then became ashes and life dull and unlivable.

I feel very close to the essential or to being when, in the aura of a luminous morning on which everything gives the appearance of being, I open my eyes at that very moment as if for the first time, and filled with astonishment I ask myself: "What is this? Where am I?" and then: "Why this, who am I, what am I doing here?"

The question can have no answer of course, but I do not expect any answer. I feel an unlimited joy, a joy "without justification" at the very moment that the question suddenly arises within me, and this joy, this exaltation seems to me to be the answer to the question that has just arisen. I feel sad, bitter, empty when I am not at the heart of the essential mystery and when I do not question myself, I mean to say, rather, when the question doesn't come up by itself, welling up from within me. It is light that makes this question arise, and this insoluble question nonetheless has an answer; it is the light itself. The question: "Where am I? Who am I?" disorients me, dislocates objects, and at the same time makes me whole at the very deepest level of myself; it is joy, the certainty of being, that takes no account of the fact that the question cannot have an answer, all the answers being outside the question, to one side of it, the question itself being the answer as if it were my own echo answering. I am completely overwhelmed, stupefied by the certainty that I am, happy on account of this gift that might not have been (everything might not have been), supremely happy, for since *this* exists there is no danger that it will cease to exist. These moments must be like moments of grace; the rest of the time questions (and not *the* question) and problems wander about in the labyrinth or the forest of definitions, of emotions, of the echoes of the voices of others. A question that arises spontaneously is an ineffable guarantee: answers can only limit it, distort it, disfigure it, suppress it. An answer that would be greater and more powerful still would be like a single total question, a blinding astonishment that would dissolve us in light.

: : :

If I suddenly halt in the middle of things, in the middle of people, if I raise my head toward the sky, or if I stare at the wall, or if I look at the ground or at my hand, writing or not writing, and if I say, very attentively: "What is that?" if I look around me and say aloud: "What is all this? Who am I, where am I, what is a question?" suddenly a blinding light invades everything, dislocates what is "understood," blots out the shadows of politics, for example, and every other shadow and everything that impels us to imagine distinctions, meanings. I can no longer ask myself the question: "What is society?" I can't even ask myself: "What train must I take to go to Prague?" for I cannot get beyond the first question, which is so powerful that it rejects everything and propels me, tears me apart, takes me to pieces, dissolves me—me and everything else. Only an insane love without an object can remain intact in the fire and the blinding light of the question; this question itself is burned up in the light that transforms it into a euphoria that has no rhyme nor reason.

: : :

I cannot be astonished enough, I don't have a large enough capacity for astonishment, my astonishment wears itself out and I cannot ask enough: "How is this possible, how in the world is this possible?"

: : :

There was a time, long, long ago, when the world seemed to man to be so charged with meanings that he didn't have *time* to ask himself questions, the manifestation was so spectacular. The whole world was like a theater in which the elements, the forests, the oceans and the rivers, the mountains and the plains, the bushes and each plant played an incomprehensible role that man tried to understand, tried to explain to himself, and gave an explanation of. But the explanations were less important: what was essential, what was satisfying, was the evidence of the presence of the gods, it was plenitude, everything was a series of glorious epiphanies. The world was full of meaning. The Apparition was nourished by the spirit of the gods, of what can be called gods; the world was dense. Exactly when did the gods retire from the world, exactly when did the images lose their color? Exactly when was the world emptied of substance, exactly when were the signs no longer signs, exactly when did the tragic break take place, exactly when were we abandoned to ourselves, that is to say, exactly when did the gods no longer want to stage a spectacle, exactly when did they no longer want us as spectators, as participants? We were left to ourselves, to our solitude, to our fear, and the problem was born. What is this world? Who are we?

: : :

A liberating state of emptiness. Something like a purification; I was like a vessel that had been emptied and cleaned: but emptied so as to be filled with fresh water. This hasn't happened.

I was aware of a freedom and I was aware of astonishment, of being astonished at this freedom. There has never been plenitude again. The light has not completely gratified me, has not inhabited me. I have merely caught a glimpse, only a glimpse.

: : :

"After a certain point, one can no longer turn back; it is this point that must be reached" (Kafka's private journal).

But at the very moment that I had only one more step to take in order to pass beyond this point of no return, I was overcome by great hesitation and there was something like a dizzy spell and then there was an agonizing, enormous regret, the call of the whole world breathing me in: voices, arms that were too gentle, the entire universe became gentle, there were soft colors and then a sort of music and then a well-being and then a softness and then something like a promise of sensual pleasure, an indescribably enveloping force dragged me down. It was as if I were afraid of being cut in two. A pain, a wound, a tear that I could not bear. I let myself fall. I capitulated. The regrets, the lead weight, had been twice as strong, or ten times as strong as the force breathing me in. It was after this regression, or, rather, this fall, that my spiritual life was interrupted, or perhaps kept waiting. I had the impression that I was now lower down, a few degrees lower down than before.

Soon not regrets but remorse tormented me, absolute nostalgia again troubled me. In fact, it was only an obscure remorse, a sort of uneasy conscience, an inner weight. The soft lights, and the arms that had pulled at me, and the colors and a whole world that promised pleasures and this whole concatenation of beings and things, this whole world was not just leaden clouds, a thick fog I wandered in, finding it painful to breathe. Even today, after so long, after so many years, absolute nostalgia sometimes puts me to the test, cruelly, but at the same time the moment that this nostalgia awakens within me it is combated by the earthly regrets that appear as soon as the other nostalgia is suddenly aroused, as before, and medusas lock me in their embrace.

Today it seems to me that the necessary trajectory is a descent, it is no longer a climb as it once was: I had the impression at that time that I had to get rid of a lead garment in order to go upward; today it seems to me that I must go back down into the suffocating depths and get to the other side of them. But today, as then, the point at which one can no longer turn back is always surrounded by this very strong, very cruel light, the cold glitter of sword blades. It is an unbearable, nonhuman light.

: : :

In his private journal Kafka also says: "If you were walking on a flat terrain and when you wanted to go forward you went backward, it is at this point that the situation would be desperate, but since you are trying to scale a hill that seems from below to be as vertical as you yourself are, the steps you retrace are due only to the conformation of the terrain and you have no reason to despair."

This is very reassuring. There is no reason to despair. It is solely the fault of the configuration of the terrain.

: : :

There is desire, there is false pride, there is fear. If there were no desire, no fear, no pride, there would be no history. Desire becomes so great that it turns into greed. It is enough, it would be enough, it should be enough to be conscious of being here, surrounded by creation and dazzled by epiphanies. Along with a taste for poverty, we have lost the possibility of contemplation. Economic problems, hatred, and disgust would not exist if there were poverty, if there were no false pride. This is not saying anything new, of course, but this is so rarely said that it becomes a brand-new thought. "Organizations" are arbitrary, as if they were outside the world. Anybody can say "nothing is important," "all is vanity," but these words are nothing but clichés, what everyone says without being aware of it, without really remembering. Anybody can also say "we lose ourselves in the multiple," but this too is a formula.

But here is what happens. I discover these truths myself at this moment. It is as if no one had ever said this to me; it is a revelation, a discovery. I remember, though doubtless I will forget in an hour, or will forget tomorrow, I remember, I understand that I am a being, a man, in the center of the world and I see the sky and I am aware that I see these streets, and I am aware that I exist, or rather I become aware that I *am*. It is being that fills me with joy and amazes me, being astonishes me much more than existing. I am stronger than nothingness. All the rest is insignificant: where can one go to seek triumphs, or seek a happiness stronger than joy, the unbelievable beatitude of existence? To live outside of contemplation in action, in hope, is stupidity and blindness. Stupidity exists however, and so even the existence of stupidity fills me with astonished amazement, full of joy. The light, the fact of being in the world. One cannot go farther. In real, essential knowledge wars and sciences, economy and architecture, poverty or wealth, hierarchies, the world divided into nations, administration, religion, action, philosophies disappear like shadows in the face of this unique and happily overwhelming reality: I exist, I am, and when I think of that everything falls silent and anything else becomes nonsense. Or else everything becomes an extravagant fete, death itself vanishes like a puff of smoke, and only insane love can embrace this satisfaction, this unheard-of joy of existing.

I have the key to happiness: remember, be profoundly, profoundly, totally conscious that you are.

I myself, sorry to say, hardly ever use this key. I keep losing it.

: : :

The feeling that we find ourselves in a past whose only roots are in forgetfulness. The thought that it is as if our existence had never been, that it is like figures erased by a sponge on a blackboard where they leave no trace, so that no one realizes that they have existed. It is as if our existence were retroactively canceled out the very moment that it began to be; this thought seems to me to be just as true today as what I once thought, one day full of light, just as true as what I was certain of then: "since I am, I am eternal." I might not have been, but since I am, since we are, there is no more danger of not being.

: : :

I find this page too: It is cold outside. In the house the red armchairs, the high-backed chairs, the tapestry, the books full of wisdom, the little tables with drawers and lace doilies are there, arranged for comfort and giving off a sort of warmth. The objects in the room seem to be breathing.

I have a calm joy, a silent harmony, a slight tipsiness; something has happened, I am somewhere else, in a place that I have been moved to with the furniture and the house. I look at the snow through the window. The street has changed. The sidewalks are white. The climbing plant on the wall across the street, the locksmith's house is silver; the young girl, our neighbor, is walking along very fast, in ski pants, with her hands in her pockets. A dog is hurrying along too.

It is the beginning of March. What with this sky, it's as if it were December again, just before Christmas. It is Christmas again. Time is therefore reversible, I say to myself, and my soul sings a silent hymn.

Where am I? In what distant province? In what century? In an old city in the mountains? At Curtea-de-Arges? Perhaps in an old English city? I am certainly in an unreal city, a city that is an island surrounded by the ocean of history, but sheltered from it. Let us not move. Let us wait for the festivities. Let us not get swallowed up. Perhaps I am going to escape. Perhaps this morning will last forever. Perhaps beyond my well-heated room and the street covered with snow, centuries have passed and are still passing, perhaps men are living in another civilization, while we remain suspended above duration, above the flow of time, above the abysses.

(This young girl passing by eternally with her hands in her pockets, or so it seemed: what has become of her since she crossed the street more than twenty years ago?)

: : :

I am lost in the thousands of words and unsuccessful acts that are "my life," which take my soul apart and destroy it. This life is between me and myself, I bear it along between me and myself, I do not recognize it as mine, and yet it is to this life that I ask to be revealed. How can you be revealed by what hides you? How can you make all the masks become transparent, how can you go back up the river of chance, of error, of disorientation, to reach the pure source? How can I correct everything that has put me in a false light? And how, with the aid of words, can I express everything that words hide? How can I express what is inexpressible?

I aspire to the impossible, I want my words to be transparent. Thousands and thousands of words, masks and lies and erring ways will have to say what the word hides. All that remains for me to do is to give the lie to each spoken word by taking it apart, by making it explode, by transfiguring it. It cannot be said that what I propose to do is easy. It cannot be said that it is intelligible either, but this no longer has any meaning at the moment that *it is no longer impos-*

sible. As a matter of fact, I don't understand myself very well, for I am the victim of words, I am dragged along, carried away by the flood of words.

As a matter of fact, I find it hard to understand what I wanted to say; or rather, I find it hard to understand what I "felt"; it is obvious that if I spoke in these terms such a long time ago of life and words and signs and an "I" that becomes another, I was clearly trying to describe my lived experience, the experience of being lost in the world, separated, lost in language and in my own language that I no longer felt to be mine but rather that of others. At present, new thinkers tell us that "it is language that speaks and not man or a man"; is this the same experience? Heidegger too tells us that being or a being is "unauthentified" by a certain social experience, and therefore by a common language; he is lost in the impersonal world of the "one"; it is necessary, therefore, to put everything in question again, it is necessary therefore to reconsider the very basis of speech, to go back to the axioms; this, it seems to me, is the task that all philosophers have taken upon themselves. But each new system of expression, once it has been adopted by others, once it has become a convention, or an acquisition, or a cliché, or an ideology, loses its essential truth. Life becomes a word. As I am not a philosopher, this happened for me on the level of affectivity, of an emotional reaction. It nonetheless seems to me that art is only able to give "a purer meaning to the words of the tribe," as Mallarmé put it. In fact, every work of art is the materialization of an almost indescribable personal experience, it is putting a language in question again, it is a rediscovery or a discovery of the world, seen by the poet for the first time. The poet cannot invent new words every time, of course. He uses the words of the tribe. But the handling of the word, the accent, a new articulation, renew them. The reader or the hearer or the contemplator of the work must in turn be able to receive this new virginity that he gives to expression.

All I do is lose my way. But I have a chance to find myself again if I keep retracing my footsteps, instead of taking the first step, if I return to the explosion of the first image, there where words express nothing but light. I find myself again, and understand myself only where words, faces, figures, walls, myself are no longer to be understood, where sounds are strangers and strange, with meanings dislocated by a very powerful light in which definitions and forms melt, like the shadow that makes light disappear. It is from this silence that speech is born again.

: : :

I say to myself: I find myself in a past that can only be found in forgetfulness now. That is to say: it is as if we had never been. We will have been like figures that the sponge will have erased on the blackboard that keeps no trace of what was written on it; no one can find out if there was something there or not. Worse still: our existence will have been canceled out retroactively, as if nothingness could devour everything by proceeding backward from our end to our beginning. We still have never been.

This feeling alternates within me with the certainty that at other times tells me that since we are we cannot not be; or else we might not be, but since we are, there is no danger that we will cease to be. A feeling of eternity.

: : :

When I want to tell the story of my life, it is a wandering that I tell of. I speak of a limitless forest, or of a wandering in a limitless forest. It is not of myself that I speak, for I look for myself with words which are made only to make me fail to find myself and which only increase the sense of being lost. I can say only these words, but even so I can tell of my essential nostalgia, and that too is very difficult, for profound desire forgets what it desires, and is degraded and lost, and breaks up into separate desires. Either the abstract word or the concrete realities of the acts that have falsified you, that have separated you from yourself are substituted for the ineffable song. We are all looking for something of extraordinary importance whose nature we have forgotten; I am writing the memoirs of a man who has lost his memory. The awareness that all the things I am saying are only substitutions will remain with me.

I therefore let myself be borne on by the flood of words. The rock appears only for a second, on rare occasions.

Only a cry can be heard in this thick fog.

When silence returns again, let the light of this cry not be forgotten.

: : :

Then again, we can meet ourselves only at an unexpected bend in the road.

: : :

Walls collapsed, definitions were dislocated. There was no longer any direction. The names of things drew apart from things. I was submerged in an ocean of blue light, I myself was nothing now but a vague luminous contour. No more form, no more shadows, no more colors, our reality broke up into thousands of pieces, went up in smoke, then the smoke also blew away, and there was nothing now but this immense sun going from one horizon to another.

Everything that I had thought to be solidly built was only castles of cards that had tumbled down. Stone was only water and fog. The world, made one, came out of a multiplicity of drawers. For everything up to that point had been only a dislocated series of boxes and contents of boxes. A priest: a box; a house: a box; an apple: a box; a passion: a box; a sensation: a box.

The impossible was coming into being. Where was I, who was I? I was a stranger and alone, infinitely a stranger to myself. I was waking up or being born in a new universe, a completely different universe, not only a universe that had been washed but a universe that had been tidied up. The stupefaction was so great that it canceled out all fear and this stupefaction was only an echo of plenitude, and what was strange immediately was transformed into what was familiar. The world was new and familiar, surprising, known, recognized, rediscovered. How shall I put it?—a world freed of this meaning; how shall I put it?—a sort of living respiration of which I was a part.

This lasted only a few instants and when "this" went away it was as if the world had been extinguished. I went back into the night or into the shadow, I bumped against objects, against walls. I was there laboriously lighting the candle of everyday comprehension whose light is only a shadow. The nightmare of this world began over and over again.

: : :

Since I have been writing plays that are staged, I have not managed to get used to errors of interpretation, either those of the "interpreters" that actors are, or the false interpretation of the critics or of the public.

I always want to be "understood," that is to say, I want people to fully understand what I tried to say since I tried to say it. A work for the theater is not a speech to the public; I therefore detest it when actors address the audience, unless it's to give an example of what should not be done and to parody didactic actors.

However, while a theatrical work is an object, a construction, a society, a whole world, it is also something that must be deciphered, be understood, that is to say, one ought to understand very well what its characters mean, say, do. And one can manage to understand eventually; incommunicability does not exist if one does not want it to exist, if one does not want to cheat. It is true that people with doctor's degrees, people from the École Normale can no longer understand, for they understand only through "systems" and tie everything to "systems" of thought, corpuses of ready-made ideas, different grids that prevent them, in a way that is almost completely natural, from embracing everything "different" that someone wants to say.

This "someone" is sociologized *before* he is understood, whereas nothing prevents him from being sociologized *afterward*. But then no one has the time.

: : :

And what right do you have to get others to incarnate your dreams, to materialize your images; what right do you have to invent characters and worlds? Are fictions "true"? They are so true that only literature, poetry, painting, and theater are engaged in down through the ages in all corners of the earth. One speaks only of imaginary characters, one writes a little literature and more literature about literature and literature about the literature of literature.

Works on psychology, psychoanalysis, sociology, metaphysics, esthetics, of course, and the philosophy of culture are almost all based on works of the imagination.

: : :

I often have insomnia. I open my eyes in the shadows. But these shadows are like a different kind of clarity, a negative light. It is in this black light that the revelation of "disaster," of "catastrophe," of "the irremediable," of "absolute failure" comes to me, with the undeniable evidence of fact. Everything seems lost to me.

Childhood is the world of miracle or of magic: it is as if creation rose luminously out of the night, all new and fresh and astonishing. Childhood is over the moment that things are no longer astonishing. When the world gives you a feeling of "déjà vu," when you are used to existence, you become an adult. The fairyland world, the brand-new marvel becomes a banality, a cliché. To be driven from childhood is to be driven from paradise, it is to be an adult. You keep the memory, the nostalgia of a present, of a presence, of a plenitude that you try to rediscover by every possible means. Rediscover it or the compensation. I have been tortured, and still am, both by the fear of death, the horror of emptiness, and by the ardent, impatient, pressing desire to live. Why does one want to live, what does "living" mean? I have waited to live. When one wants to live, it is no longer a sense of wonder that one is seeking but in its stead, since only childhood or a simple and superior lucidity can attain it, what one seeks is to be sated. One never is; one cannot be. Material things are not life. One can't manage to live. This "will to live" means nothing.

I had sought a false path to salvation, I gave myself bad directions.

: : :

I envy schoolteachers of a time not long ago in little provincial towns. Streets with trees, a river. Nice pupils. The café. The restaurant. The wine. The afternoon nap. The sunny days. The books. The teachers chatted after class, strolling down the streets of the town. Tipping their hats to the right, to the left. In the evening they got drunk. A sort of paradise.

: : :

Panic again.

: : :

The panic of three days ago is over, things have calmed down again for the moment.

: : :

I was not yet twelve. I had been sent to spend my vacation at my uncle Alexandre's, my mother's brother, who was twenty-three and had tuberculosis and died two years later at the age of twenty-five. He had been sent there himself to look after his health. The ground floor apartment that I lived in in Paris, in the rue de l'Avre with my mother and my grandparents, was damp, bleak, and dark. Alexandre lived in an immense country house in the little town. In reality it was a little country town, half-provincial, half-suburban; the house had a great many rooms and an immense attic above the third floor which smelled of apples.

To me, it was a castle; I ran up and down the stairs all day long, I explored the house, there was wallpaper, it wasn't like it was in Paris; the house had the sadness of houses that are not familiar to us, a sadness and also a mystery or a magic, something that was at once attractive and repellent. But the mornings were brand new: another sun, another light, not the same noises. Unknown people, new people walked in the streets that were brand new to me and then there was the road, white and pink, with little houses along it. Alexandre worked, coughing the while; I took walks all by myself and explored. Once, beneath a very blue sky, I went to the end of the village and beyond, I was in a field of wheat, with the steeple of the little village in the distance; then I found myself on the little public square opposite the church; the square was almost empty; how beautiful it was! A little universe, all fresh and clean that seemed to have appeared, that seemed to have been born that very morning, like a baby.

: : :

The Socialist idea of progress comes from religion. Thus Christians believe that our world is a fallen world, and man a fallen creature who is to regain paradise after he has passed stages of suffering, of passion, of purification. Revolutionaries also think that humanity will be "saved" after necessary wars, upheavals, dictatorships, and terror. This, in short, is what progress is. That materialists can believe in progress seems to me to represent a contradiction on their part. Progress is a mystical idea. Why should there be progress? What does this progress consist of? What are we heading toward? If the materialists were consistent, they should not think of the achievement of perfect humanity except in terms of its being identical with the laws of matter, in terms of the achievement of a society that would function like celestial mechanics, or biology, without any possibility of error or divergence. The Socialists are religious men who are unaware of their religiosity; they adopt the myths of religious men in forms that are only slightly different. For what drives us toward progress, what drives us toward perfection, and what is perfection?

July 1967: I see in the paper the photograph of the Russian admiral commanding the Soviet fleet in the Mediterranean, which at present is lying off the shore of Israel. He is enormous, powerful, with more stripes than a general under Napoleon III, hyperdecorated, the hard look on his face the very symbol of power. He is absolute authority. For me, this is the very face of tyranny, this is the cop that all the French intellectuals detest in their country. But, they say, this isn't the face of tyranny, it is the personification of the dictatorship of the proletariat. Since they have given another name to tyranny, since they have found an excuse, a conscious justification for it, they throw themselves at the feet of the tyrant and can calmly let his boots trample them. What can they do? The "intellectuals" won't permit any obstacle to be placed in the way of their freedom in their own country, but in fact there are no such obstacles, because power allows itself to be discussed and attacked, because power does not exist, and it would seem that this is what they detest: the absence of real authority, the nonpower. Otherwise they would not like tyranny and its boots when it manifests itself in such a real, such an "objective," such a gigantic, such an ogrelike way. Not everyone likes tyranny, or else he only half likes it. But there is cowardice. Why fight something so strong, so invincible? Why detest this tyranny, that is to say, why put oneself in a state of psychological discomfort?

If I pretended to like what I detest, I would detest less, I would perhaps love, I would let myself go, I would let myself be raped, I would end up adoring. All I need say is that I am not vanquished by the ogre, that the ogre is not an ogre but love, that he is beneficent revolution. That's the way out of the difficulty. That's the way tyrants get accepted.

When intellectuals, writers, artists come from the countries of the East, eager for freedom, the lack of understanding of people in the West astonishes them and makes them despair. They are not astonished any longer, for now they know. They have been preached at enough, and scolded enough: what's this, they are told, you got rid of capitalism and lived in a Socialist country and still you complain! Certain of them have even been denounced by Paris leftists who could not live one week in the countries where the new tyrants prevail. For obviously everything is ambiguous and somewhat contradictory: they both love and detest tyranny. No Sartre, no Simone de Beauvoir could put up with presenting their texts to committees of adjutants or generals in uniform. Thus the intellectuals of the Eastern countries make a lonely effort, amid the lack of understanding of the intellectuals in the West, to earn a bit of freedom little by little: to be allowed to do nonfigurative painting, to be allowed to speak of love, of their happiness, of their unhappiness in their books, rather than of tomorrows that sing or bawl collectively; when they have managed to stage a play that is a little bit freer, one of the so-called avant-garde plays, they are quite happy. They talk of love, they talk of the beauty of the world, they criticize, they become more human—and they are put in prison. In France a whole new body of criticism, which prevails in the theater among other places, is trying to suppress freedom. That is to say, everything that the authority of the State does in Russia, all the mechanism of State censorship is in the hands of the opposition in France, or is its ideal. We have a liberal State and a censorship by a literally authoritarian opposition. This is the reaction of petits bourgeois who think they are revolutionaries and are possessed by the demon of power. On the other hand, the spirit of intellectuals in Russia and elsewhere is liberal. It is an oppressed and persecuted liberalism, but it is a real and genuine liberalism.

But what can this spirit of freedom and nonconformism do? What are its weapons? At the last international congress of writers in Moscow, the Russian "writers" who talked the loudest, or who talked at all, were generals in uniform or admirals, policemen. One might almost wish that adjutants in uniform would speak out forcefully, and bang on the table, at all meetings of French or English writers to teach them how to live.

Around 1940: The Vice-President of the Council has attacked the Hungarians in a violent speech because the Hungarians are insulting the Romanians in their papers. All this
has to do with Transylvania, of course. Our neighbor,
Judge V., who beats his maids and fires them without having
paid them their wages—he has done this with seven maids
in a year and nothing can be done since he is a magistrate
—turns on his radio and the voice of the Vice-President
can be heard through the walls. The words are incomprehensible, but I notice that his voice is an imitation of Hitler's. The Vice-President is not a Nazi, of course, and it is
out of necessity that he goes along with the Germans in
opposing Russia, in the justified hope of getting back Bessarabia, which Russia has unjustly annexed. The Vice-President is not a Hitlerite, yet he has been Hitlerized, so to
speak; he screams, then his voice grows softer, then it becomes strident again, then he screams again, then he in-
dulges in pathetic declamation. How is this speech possible?
It is because the Hungarians do not want to send any more
divisions to the Russian front. Then the Germans blackmail
the Hungarians by making use of Romania, seemingly as-
suring the Romanians that they will get back the part of
Transylvania that was ceded to the Hungarians. In actual
fact, Romania is really dismembered: Bessarbia and a
part of Bukovina are occupied by the Russians, half of
Transylvania is in the hands of the Hungarians, and all the
young people of the country are dying in the war.

I can still hear the voice of the Vice-President of the
Council speaking in the new style for political discourses,
the style and the intonations of Hitler, and among the
screams I hear a few words here and there: "The two
columns that can stay up without the vault . . . but the
vault cannot stay up without the columns . . . the vault
rises from the columns again . . ." It is no longer men

speaking but dogs barking. Hitler has a hoarse voice. The Vice-President of the Romanian Council thinks that he has to have a hoarse voice too. But he's not very good at being hoarse. It is a fake hoarse voice.

: : :

Yesterday the teachers were very upset. The natural science teacher, who had listened to part of the speech in the office of the school, comes running into the faculty room shouting: "The government is finally taking a stand; our army is going to reconquer Transylvania!" The teacher was dangerously overexcited. I quickly went back to class and calmly gave a French lesson to my little students who were very nice yesterday. At least when I am doing that I don't hear the speeches, nor the speeches about the speeches, and I have the impression that everything is passing by to one side of me: the demonstrations and the processions, and the military ceremonies, and the killing, and the filthy stupidity of the world. Yesterday there was a demonstration at the faculty of law, in front of my apartment windows: there were Romanian, German, Japanese flags, but I had to teach five hours at the lycée yesterday and left home early. I went gaily past the faculty of law, happy to think that I would not see either the cars or the battalions arrive, that I would not see the flags in the wind, or the excited crowd that day, and that I would be far away from this spectacle staged by the Germans. For, as we know, nothing can happen that is not contrived by the Germans. I wasn't completely at ease at the lycée however. Coming out of class at one o'clock, the natural science teacher gave us a little speech about the Vice-President's speech. He had liked the orator's expression "My very dear, beloved students," very much, and also the mention of "our beloved nation" (the word "nation" ought to disappear from the dictionary).

And then the teachers commented on the rumors that Romanian and German troops had already entered Hungary. I must say that the majority of the teachers went wild: "Is it true that the armies have entered Transylvania?" they said. "Ah, if this were really true, if only this were true!" hesitant and hypocritical voices said, but their faces were pale. None of them want Transylvania to be reconquered by the new government, neither the Anglophiles, who want Transylvania to be won back by the English, nor the Iron Guards, who want to take back Transylvania themselves, rather than let the Vice-President do so. At present the reconquest of Transylvania would be a disaster for either of them. Yet they are all good patriots. As they left, the Anglophiles consoled each other: "The Germans will not want to . . . they don't want to see the English and their allies . . ." And the Iron Guards consoled each other: "The Germans will not let the Antonesco government do that. In reality they'll give this gift to us Iron Guards."

: : :

Teachers are badly paid, for everything goes to the army and the police. I give French lessons at home. Yesterday I earned quite a tidy sum; then I went to the barber's; it was a nice day, the sun and the light streamed in through the big windows of the barber shop. Leaving . . . Am I still young enough? . . . Looking at myself in the mirror, I saw that the hair on the top of my head is getting thinner.

: : :

A German conspiracy in Hungary. The Wehrmacht has intervened. The Hungarian Nazis (the "Arrows of Fire") are in power. The news is not completely confirmed. Antonesco's government is in a fix. How can they find a way out? They are a government of the center. A plot by the Germans and the Iron Guards threatens them too. What are they going to do to try to neutralize the extremist elements on the right? This Romanian government goes along with the Germans, but it is really composed of people from the center and the moderate left. They will have to appeal to the Germans and to Hitler himself to support them against the Iron Guards from the outside, and to thwart the powerful Iron Guard inside the country they are going to try to get the support of the anti-Nazis, of all the democrats, with the exception of the Communists of course; in any case, this latter party has no more than a few hundred members.

: : :

As might be expected, France seems lost, the French give the appearance of being snuffed out under our very eyes; from time to time they still grumble vaguely like people whose sleep is disturbed.

Let everything collapse. I would like for there to be nothing left at all.

But does one ever know with History? History has its plans perhaps. Everything is possible; France may even be a great country once again.

: : :

The sadness of existing. The corpses piled up in the Caucasus. The travail of the ruined man in the burned cities of Russia, the misery and the fear that overwhelm the inhabitants of Russia, of Poland, of Czechoslovakia, of Yugoslavia, of Greece, of Belgium, of Norway, of Holland. The suffering of France, which to me was the fatherland of the world. The pride and the stupid insolence of the Germans, their crimes being all the more serious in that they are idiotic, the stupidity of the intelligent writers and journalists who put out anti-Judeo-Masonic, anti-Anglo-American propaganda, the fury that is madness; the dearest friends that I have left behind and who are getting along as best they can, amid war, my mother's poor wrinkled little hands that will never caress me again; and this nostalgia, this absolute thirst that will never be quenched, and then the threats that surround my person. All this disgust too, and this indescribable pain, and all this fear—and the starry abysses that fill me with anguish . . . All this can be drowned tonight in a glass of alcohol.

How can I become just a simple, selfish man? What can I do in order to be indifferent, not only intellectually but psychologically? Yes, not being able to drain the cup of remorse to the bottom, I will go drink that glass of alcohol.

: : :

I am not fighting in the war. Dying for Nazism would be senseless. Fighting for Stalin and Russian imperialism? That would be just as stupid. (*Eight hundred thousand Romanian soldiers died in the war against the Russians, then, when Romania had reversed its alliances, five hundred thousand more died in the war against Germany. When they were at war against the Soviets, the Romanians were fighting for the King of Prussia, for the occupant. When they turned against Germany, they fought for the Soviets who took two Romanian provinces after the war, occupied the country, and liquidated the intellectual elite, both on the left and on the right.*)

I find myself in France, which is my real country because it is the country of my childhood, sheltered, even though this shelter is precarious and threatened; I don't dare stick my head out, but I am happy not to be duped. A few governments, a few groups, a few committees, a few general staffs lead the masses of humanity to their murder. The Revolution? I haven't believed in it since Stalin delivered the German Communists who had taken refuge in Russia over to

Hitler. I haven't believed in it since Stalin, that foul Czar, has been at the head of the Russians. If I can't be among the leaders, among those who allow themselves to send others to their death, I can at least arrange things so as not to be sent to my death by them. Acting? I am too lucid to do so. Since people keep struggling, there is action—for those who like it. Those who act have a liking for death, or for power. I like only independence, I don't want to be pushed by others. Those who like risk or excitement need to find, and manage to find, theoretical justifications, but I know that nothing changes and that revolutions merely bring on tyranny, or restore tyranny. I know that there is no reason, no necessity for anything. Yesterday I still loved what are called civilized French values: they are only a threadbare humanism. I refuse to be the naive agent of formulas and conceptions that are making the rounds throughout the world. At this moment, I subjectively detest Nazism and Hitler almost as much as the fat bourgeois. Objectively I realize that I must not detest anything or anybody. I am surviving. I have the feeling that this is a sin; I must get over this guilty conscience. I am getting over it. Man will perhaps know himself better some day. Psychoanalysis will be perfected. Everything will be explained. We will laugh at ourselves. The confused impulses of our unconscious will have light thrown on them, will be dissolved, will be mastered. The world of incoherent unrest will disappear. There will be no more revolutions; collective illnesses will be cured. Perhaps people will no longer feel the need for a miraculous or supernatural world, for who knows what repressions, what obsessions provoke these desires which will not stand up under a psychoanalysis and a sociology that have been perfected. If there are no longer to be these sorts of psychological illnesses, what is called inner life will disappear. Art will become useless. Men will become functionaries of the cosmos, will become one with their function in the universe, they will be as perfect as the stars, and their movements will be those of celestial mechanics. We will live without hope and without purpose, but our function will require neither hope nor doubt. Human consciousness will expand, will dilate to such a point that it will finally merge with cosmic laws and disappear.

: : :

In 1936 the left represented freedom, humanism, generosity. The Popular Front was absolutely necessary in order to confront the different ideologies that were the enemies of freedom, enemies of men who were at once prideful and crude in their fierce stupidity: a large proportion of European intellectuals, from France to Germany, from Italy to Hungary and Romania, naturally were marching in "the direction of History," which was tending to the right. Not all of them, fortunately. There was the Popular Front to oppose the Action Française, the sclerosis of the heart of the fat bourgeois, the various odious Iron Guards.

It should perhaps be noted that neither Sartre, nor Jean Genet, nor Simone de Beauvoir lent their luster to this movement, but that others, such as André Malraux, were leftists. Nazism collapsed. But tyranny has survived. No French intellectual would be willing to live a week under the orders of the Chinese leaders or in Stalinist or post-Stalinist Russia. Tyranny today comes from the left. And today we see that the same intellectuals or their sons who were once rightist progressivists have become leftist progressivists, that is to say antiprogressivists. Obviously it is not the Socialist idea that is in question here, and I am convinced that Poland, Hungary, Romania, Bulgaria, and Czechoslovakia could have built Socialism and a world of joy instead of being obliged to set up sub-Soviet tyrannies in their countries at the behest of the foul Russian tyranny. One cannot hold this against Socialism, but one can also not forgive the Russians for having disfigured and diverted it.

Two Soviet writers have recently been arrested, imprisoned, and brought to trial for holding the wrong opinions. There has been no protest in France, except for a few lines in the *Figaro littéraire* and in the review *Esprit*. One organization, however, the PEN Club, which was set up to defend the freedom of culture, does exist in France, and its leaders, being bureaucrats, get along far better with the bureaucrats of repressive totalitarian parties and regimes than they do with the suffering poets in these countries who are the defenders of freedom and whom the people on the French left refuse to understand, with a total scorn for the "human" they claim to be the partisans of (why disturb the comfort, the junkets, the bureaucratic advantages of the PEN Club, why open a breach in their selfish serenity and well-conceived interests?), whereas these poets opposed to the regime are the only real leftists, the only people in whom people with a heart, which is rightist, can place their hope.

We are told today that freedom, generosity, progress lie on the left. In this way, the enemies of freedom, of generosity, of love, of human sympathy can have an easy conscience, as can the unconscious members of the Nobel Prize jury who, after having given the prize to the great hero Pasternak, subsequently dared to award it to the valet of dictatorships, Sholokhov, or to Sartre, the advocate of tyrannies, both of whom hid behind the mask of "noble" sentiments.

The right, certainly, has not become the left. It is not very likable. But it is certain that the left embodies a more dangerous, fiercer spirit, possessed as it is by the need for tyranny, the need of angry petits bourgeois, the need of those who march along with history, the opportunists of all the rights, all the lefts in history.

: : :

Sometimes, in April, there are limpid mornings, with a gentle, very fragile grace. It seems as if the universe has just been born, that it has just emerged from the original, boundless water, that it is still damp, that it retains something of the transparency of lakes. The world seems all pure and new, its light intact. All is light and water. It is the first day. The world has just emerged, it is still unreal, everything is still only an assemblage of colors, the outlines of its forms stand out, ready to be blurred. The world makes its appearance. Flowers grow out of the asphalt; fountains suddenly well up in the deserts. All the people are young, the girls walk without touching the ground. The universe becomes completely transparent, like a bride's veil. The air stirs like gentle waves. The event will perhaps occur. The only event for which the world is created. Everything is no more than an expectation, a Sunday, and this light that is at once glorious and soft looks like a party dress. The great hope. A calm comes into being in the light and one hears the vibrations of the bells that are about to ring, organs barely hold back their sounds, the bows of violins are about to play. All the voices await the signal to sing the triumphal hymn. But the waiting is prolonged and the whole universe is now only arms stretched out. The white bird is as motionless as the sky, the trees by the houses hold their breath to hear the announcement of the event. Will there be an outburst of joy? All eyes are fixed on the horizon to

catch the moment when the light will melt into a greater
light . . .

: : :

Yes, beauty is agonizing because it is only a phantom, or
because it is outside myself, or because it does not belong
to me. It awakens in me the nostalgia for an essential absence, it reminds me that I do not have, that I am not, that
I am not, that I do not have.

If astonishment is something like an illumination, like a
fire that sets me ablaze, beauty does not penetrate me: between me and the luminous universe that appears to me there
is something like a transparent, inflexible, hard wall. Beauty
is like an inaccessible light that surrounds me but escapes
me, and I am only a dark shadow in its splendor. It is a
mirage. In fact, this is exactly what it is: it gives rise to unbearable nostalgia, insatiable hunger and thirst.

: : :

The starry sky. The blue sea. This white, immaculate city
of the South, rising from the plain. A cathedral in the sunlight. The sun-drenched hair of this woman. These paintings
and this music. These forms that are too pure. This limpid-
ity, this transparency, all these colors. All this merely tears
the dark veils of my everyday life. Oh, I would rather that
nothing appear to me, I prefer not to hear anything, I prefer to take refuge in the lukewarm, bearable grayness of
sleepiness and forgetfulness. But I cannot prevent myself
from being overcome by infinite desire.

: : :

Beauty is a precarious trace that eternity causes to appear to us and that it takes away from us. A manifestation of
eternity, and a sign of death as well. Often it seems to me to
be an evil flower of nothingness, or else the cry of the world
as it dies, or a desperate, sumptuous prayer.

And then ashes.

The light has blinded me. But it has stopped me. Otherwise I would not be here writing, and suffering from wanting to remember this event which in any case can never be forgotten.

: : :

Astonishment made the world seem both strange and close to me. Beauty makes the world seem strange to me. Beauty makes me jealous. Astonishment wholly satisfies me. Memory has something of the nature of beauty, something of the nature of astonishment. Everything that seemed painful, unbearable to me, the most terrible events acquired a beauty and a strangeness in my memory. Astonished as I confront the world, I say to myself: "Is this possible?" And this transfiguration of the reality of everyday life that becomes a glorious reality carries me away, and I myself feel transfigured. Astonishment is like a total illumination that leaves no corner of space for shadow. Beauty causes only a part of the world, "in which I am not," to emerge, relegating the rest of the world, and myself, to the shadows. I stand to one side and look at a treasure that gleams in the darkness of a cavern.

The light of memory, or rather the light that memory lends to things, is the palest light of all. But something that one remembers nonetheless seems to suddenly emerge from a sort of night of forgetfulness, a sort of nothingness.

: : :

I am not quite sure whether I am dreaming or remembering, whether I have lived my life or dreamed it. Just as dreams do, memory makes me profoundly aware of the unreality, the evanescence of the world, a fleeting image in the moving water, colored smoke. How can everything contained within firm contours be extinguished? Reality is infinitely fragile, infinitely precarious; everything that I have found it hard to live through becomes sad and sweet. I want to hold back everything that nothing can hold back. Phantoms. I am a snowman that is melting. I slip away, I can't hold back, I separate from myself. I am farther and farther away, a silhouette and then a black dot.

The world is about to freeze. A polar insensibility has already begun to cover us over. And then there is going to be a huge sun that will melt these blocks of ice, and after that there will be vapor, then the fog itself will fade away in the blue light. There will no longer be the slightest trace.

: : :

Alas, all the sincerity, all the authenticity, all the truth, everything that I have lived and felt all by myself is already disappearing in clichés, expressions that belong to the public patrimony and to men in general.

There is no individual who is completely alone, we are told by structuralist sociologists. The individual's whole psychology comes from the outside, from society, from the drives and counterdrives of the whole. He is thus only a pawn on a chessboard. He has no value except in relation to the whole. The individual is thus said to be an illusion. He doesn't exist. He isn't anything.

It is not only the studies of archaic societies that have made us aware of this, but also, certainly, modern totalitarianisms.

However, whatever position she may find herself in on the chessboard, the queen will play her role as queen. Wherever he is, the pawn or the knight or the king will only be pawns, knights, or kings and will play, or be made to play, their game or their role as pawn or knight.

Within the whole of the collectivity, I myself am a madman, for example. I am made to play my part of course. I can play my part in the game only as a madman. Unlike what happens in a game of chess, the madman * in society is aware that he is a madman. I am the madman, I know it, and I will play the game, taking into consideration the other figures in the game, my madman's game. I am obliged to be a madman, but I play with complete conscious awareness of the whole of the situation. No matter what situation I might be in, no matter if the positions change, my madness will not change. The whole is not aware that it is the whole. The individual, I, the madman, am aware of my personality as a madman. There is no consciousness of the whole. There is only individual consciousness. So it is situations that change, but my essence is unchangeable. We have always known that we were in a certain position. It is the fact that more account is being taken of this right now that is significant. But it is always I who become aware of the whole. It is an ideological mania these days to put the accent on the group. I for my part am perfectly able to place the emphasis on what is different, on what is not the others, even though it is with the others. I feel myself to be ir- reducible.

The miracle has happened. For me at least. My friends in the various ministries have gotten me a valid passport, with the proper visas. I am taking the train tomorrow. My wife is going with me. I am like an escaped prisoner who flees in the guard's uniform. I will be in France, in Lyon, Wednes- day.

---

* In French the bishop in chess is called the "madman"—*Trans- lator's note*.